I0471758

# Dialogue & Initiative

## 2012 Edition

## Special Issue on 'Occupy!'

Published by the
Committees of Correspondence Education Fund

Changemaker Publications

Dialogue & Initiative is a discussion journal published by
the Committees of Correspondence Education Fund, Inc.,

220 E 42nd St., Suite 407, New York, NY 10017-5806

(212) 868-3773

Email: national@cc-ds.org
Web: www.cc-ds.org

Editor: Harry Targ

Editorial Committee: Carl Bloice, Todd Freeberg, Pat Fry,
Michael Kaufman,Ted Pearson, Ted Reich, Meta Van Sickle

For this issue: Carl Davidson

Manuscripts not exceeding 5000 words are invited. Send
text via email; hard copy can be mailed or faxed. Manuscripts will be returned if a acompanied by postage-paid,
self-addressed packaging.

# Table of Contents

# Introduction

# Critical Force and Main Force: The Young People Occupying Are Standing Up for All of Us

## *By Carl Davidson*

The actions of hundreds of thousands of primarily young people, inspired into direct action by Occupy Wall Street in New York City's financial district, in now closing its first wave. The encampments in hundred of parks and city squares are being taken down—some by force, some by choice. How long it takes before we see a second wave of upsurge and whether the numbers and militancy will swell is anyone's guess, but expect more in May, after the weather breaks. May Day events will be held in many cities, and a national mobilization is underway to 'Occupy Chicago' in opposition to a meeting of NATO and the G8 global elites.

In this publication we have assembled some of the more interesting analysis and reporting on the OWS movement so far, together with think pieces about its future. We hope organizers find it useful in the work of revolutionary education in this interim period and beyond.

### Allies Come Forward

Most of the youth are students, but many are also unemployed and underemployed young workers. As the struggle grew, important allies came forward—many groupings of officials, staffers and activists from the trade unions, many representatives of civill rights groups and community based organizations, as well as a wide array of peace and justice coalitions. While they may not have camped out overnight, they turned out for mass actions and offered material and personal support, making their way downtown to spend a few hours helping out.

The occupying youth certainly have a just cause. While the Wall Street 'banksters' have bailed themselves out and paid themselves huge bonuses with trillions from the public treasury, these young people are saddled with a severe lack of jobs and underemployment. The students were hit with a degree of crushing debt to pay for their educations that would have been unthinkable 40 years ago. If they manage to graduate, they would still face a financial burden large enough for a home mortgage—all before they start their first full-time jobs, assuming they are lucky enough to find one that pays a living wage.

*Opening mass rally for Occupy Pittsburgh*

But these youth and students quickly fought for more than their own immediate concerns. They raised a whole range of demands—Medicare for All, defending social security, for passing the various jobs bills in Congress, opposing racism and sexism, ending the wars, and abolition of the death penalty in the wake of the recent unjust execution of Troy Davis, and hundreds more.

While still a militant minority, these radical youth are the cutting edge of a new popular front against finance capital, one expressing the interests and the aims of an emerging progressive majority.

## Moral High Ground

Young rebels often manifest a moral clarity that awakens and prods the rest of us. Through their direct actions, they become a critical force, holding up a mirror for an entire society to take a look at itself, what it has come to, and what choices lay before it. The classic and historic example is the four young African American students that sat in at a lunch counter and ordered a cup of coffee in Greensboro, North Carolina back in 1960. There are many more, not only in this country but around the world, from the students in France in 1968, to the young guerrillas of Cuba in 1959, to the youth of the Arab spring only a year ago.

The OWS protests, in this sense, as a critical force, are thus a clarion call to the trade unions, the community organizations and everyone concerned with economic and social justice. But while the youth are clearly operating as a critical force in these first waves of insurgency, when all is said and done, they are not the main force. That power resides in labor, in the working class generally and in the wider and diverse communities of the oppressed nationalities and masses of women. It's in the hands of everyone that's part of an emerging progressive majority for peace and prosperity, everyone that wants a U-Turn against the country's current path to more wars and deeper austerity.

The relationship between the critical force and the main forces is a dynamic one. They need each other, one for the audacity that awakens, the other for the more strategic power of mass organization in workplaces and neighborhoods required for both counter-hegemonic pressure and unleashing centers of dual power for deeper structural change. But its also a relationship that can be strained and frayed—by conservatism on one side and by a 'substitutionist' adventurism on the other.

Our task as part of the socialist left is to build and nurture the relation between the critical force and the main force. We have to make use of organic connections with each side of it, and approach it with openness and equity, serving as resources rather than self-appointed vanguards. It's going to take more than votes and 'business as usual' politics to push back the right wing and its Wall Street allies in 2012. It's going to take the serious 'street heat' of mass insurgency from the grassroots as well. Let's lend a hand both shaping its unity and enhancing its power with new alliances. This volume of essays and articles should fire your imaginations and light the path ahead.

*Carl Davidson is a national co-chair of CCDS.*

# The 99%: A Community of Resistance

**The Occupy movement's exhilarating potential lies in forging a unity that can make a new majority of the old minorities**

## *By Angela Davis*

When the Occupy Wall Street movement erupted on 17 September 2011, I happened to be reflecting on my remarks for the upcoming Interna-

tional Herbert Marcuse Society conference. By the time the conference convened on 27 October at the University of Pennsylvania, the encampment in Zuccotti Park was well-established and similar encampments had emerged in hundreds of communities around the country. On the opening day of the Marcuse conference, there were over 300 tents in the plaza outside Philadelphia city hall.

The organising theme of the conference - "Critical Refusals" - was originally designed to encourage us to reflect on the various ways Marcuse's philosophical theories push us in the direction of a critical political practice lo-cated outside the proper realm of philosophy, but nevertheless as an-chored in philosophy as it is in a will to transform society.

## The Marcuse Connection

So, while we were certainly prepared to ponder the connection between Marcuse's philosophical ideas and his association with the movements of the sixties, we were struck by the serendipitous affinity of the theme with the emergent Occupy movement. As presenters arrived in Philadel-phia, we repeatedly expressed our enthusiasm about the confluence of the Wall Street and Philadelphia occupations and the conference theme, which seemed to us to emphatically enact the 21st- century relevance of Herbert Marcuse's work.

I don't know whether any of us could not have predicted that on the second day of the conference, the plenary audience of over 1,000 would be so riveted by this historical conjuncture that almost all of us spontaneously joined a night march, which wended its way through the streets of Philadelphia toward the tents outside city hall. At the site, I reflected aloud - with the assistance of the human microphone - on the differences between the social movements with which we have become familiar over the last decades and this newly-grown community of resistance.

In the past, most movements have appealed to specific communities - workers, students, black people, Latinas/Latinos, women, LGBT communities, indigenous people - or they have crystallised around specific issues like war, the environment, food, water, Palestine, the prison industrial complex. In order to bring together people associated with those communities and movements, we have had to engage in difficult coalition-building processes, negotiating the recognition for which communities and issues inevitably strive.

## Community of Resistance

In a strikingly different configuration, this new Occupy Movement imagines itself from the beginning as the broadest possible community of resistance - the 99%, as against the 1%. It is a movement arrayed from the outset against the most affluent sectors of society - big banks and financial institutions, corporate executives, whose pay is obscenely disproportionate to the earnings of the 99%. It seems to me that an issue such as the prison industrial complex is already implicitly embraced by this congregation of the 99%.

Indeed, it can be persuasively argued that the 99% should move to ameliorate the conditions of those who constitute the bottom tiers of this potential community of resistance - which would mean working on behalf of those who have suffered most from the tyranny of the 1%. There is a direct connection between the pauperizing effect of global capitalism and the soaring rates of incarceration in the US. Decarceration and the eventual abolition of imprisonment as the primary mode of punishment can help us begin to revitalize our communities and to support education, healthcare, housing, hope, justice, creativity and freedom.

The Occupy activists and their supporters have brought us together as the 99%. They call upon the majority to stand up against the minority. The old minorities, in effect, are the new majority. There are major responsibilities attached to this decision to forge such an expansive community of resistance. We say no to Wall Street, to the big banks, to corporate executives making millions of dollars a year. We say no to student debt. We are learning also to say no to global capitalism and to the prison industrial complex. And even as police in Portland, Oakland and now New York, move to force activists from their encampments, we say no to evictions and to police violence.

Occupy activists are thinking deeply about how we might incorporate opposition to racism, class exploitation, homophobia, xenophobia, ableism, violence done to the environment and transphobia into the resistance of the 99%. Of course, we must be prepared to challenge military occupation and war. And if we identify with the 99%, we will also have to learn how to imagine a new world, one where peace is not simply the absence of war, but rather, a creative refashioning of global social relations.

Thus, the most pressing question facing the Occupy activists is how to craft a unity that respects and celebrates the immense differences among the 99%. How can we learn how to come together? This is something those of the 99% who are living at Occupy sites can teach us all. How can we come together in a unity that is not simplistic and oppressive, but complex and emancipatory, recognizing, in June Jordan's words that "we are the ones we have been waiting for."

Angela Davis at Occupy Philadelphia, 28 October 2011.

# Class War: Where Do We Stand?

## By Mark Solomon

When I first proposed the subject of a lecture in March, 2010 entitled "Class War: Where Do We Stand?" there was little heat on the front of class conflict (or class struggle – a stronger and more pointed term) at least on the side of the oppressed. Warren Buffett, the relatively enlightened billionaire had famously remarked: "there is class warfare and our side is winning." Political opponents of the Obama administration

were whining that the President's moderate reforms (all designed not to undermine corporate interests) were manifestations of ugly "class warfare" that was dragging the country down the road to the "Socialist European Welfare State."

On October 2, 2010 about seventy-five thousand people gathered at the Lincoln Memorial to demand a sweeping, effective federal jobs program. Leading national organizations (the AFL-CIO, NAACP, national student bodies, environmental, civic and religious groups) sponsored the rally. But there was a marked lack of sustained follow-up mobilization (the size of the crowd was compared unfavorably to an earlier Tea Party event at the same venue).

All that was going on as the country continued its rapid descent into a worsening economic crisis. From 1979 to 2007 the income of the wealthiest 1 percent of the population in the US increased 275 percent, while the income of the poorest 20 percent of the population increased by only 18 percent. in the last decade –the stock market decline, the housing bubble, the dot.com collapse, unemployment and stagnating wages drained 25 trillion dollars from the vast majority (the baby boomer generation alone has lost 25% of its net worth) while the super rich have accumulated unfathomable wealth. There are over 26 million unemployed, underemployed or exhausted and no longer seeking work. Close to half (49%) of the population are now living near the poverty line while 15% is at or below it. In addition, over three million home foreclosures have occurred; more than 50 million people live without health insurance; tens of thousands of college students are drowning in student loan debt while tuition has risen 100% in the last decade, while costs of health have rise by up to 69%; food by 156%, and gasoline up 48%.

The permanently impoverished, especially among national and racial minorities continued to struggle to be heard while the disillusioned so-called middle class has now claimed its voice, despairing the loss of the very foundation of the "American Dream" -- hope for a decent life for its members and a better life for its children. The pain behind dry statistics was recently illustrated by an anguished father who said on national public radio: "I fear that my daughter will be saddled for the rest of her life with paying off student loans; I fear that my son with an engineering degree will at best wind up working at Burger King."

All this has led the conservative publication *Business Insider* to say: "the middle class is being systematically wiped out of existence in America." (Of course the publication, echoing politicians, pundits and even labor leaders is really talking about the working class. The stubborn illusion of a broad middle stratum—that makes non-propertied workers and the poor invisible—is an ironic perpetuation of the myth of a stable, inclusive middle class society—even as that class is on the verge of being pronounced extinct.)

## Occupy is No Surprise

When one considers the gravity of the crisis, the emergence of Occupy Wall Street should have been no surprise. But it was – largely because social movements generally gestate slowly; their breakthroughs often cannot be predicted and they must generate monumental impact to get the attention of mainstream media.

Yet, the influences that would propel OWS into existence were visible and compelling. Globalization has rendered the systemic crisis of capitalism nearly universal—making resistance nearly universal. There were desperate widespread working class protests in the streets of Greece against austerity dictated by the European Union and the European Central Bank. With over 23 percent unemployment, thousands of Spanish young people, the "Indignados" filled city and town squares in relentless protests; huge worker strikes and demonstrations hit Britain and France. Of course, the dramatic, courageous "Arab Spring," that spread from Tunisia, to Egypt and in complicated, problematical form to Libya and Syria had an impact on the collective consciousness of emerging protest in the United States. In the US, determined, unprecedented fight back of workers and students in Wisconsin against a right wing governor fixated upon destroying collective bargaining set the stage for the emergence of Occupy Wall Street by affirming the power of mass dissent.

Young people, by-and-large embraced new technology, with its enormous potential to educate and mobilize. The call was originally sent out on the Internet to "occupy" Wall Street, the prime symbol and culprit of unconscionable greed that was principally responsible for running the economy into the ground. That summons to "occupy" the public space (Zuccotti Park) had an electrifying effect – echoing a somewhat forgotten tradition of encampment protest exemplified by the 1932 veterans' bonus camp at Anacostia Flats in Washington and Martin Luther King's Poor Peoples Campaign on the DC mall in 1968.

The occupiers, among them educated, skilled and long-time jobless, may not have been fully conscious at the start of the tradition embedded in the country's history of "the commons" – a place of collective (public) ownership – a space owned and shared by the entire community to be utilized for the community's interests and immune to exploitation by property-craving classes and individuals. In seizing that public space the occupiers were reaffirming the profound sense of community, caring for each other and for the homeless and mentally unstable who were drawn to the encampments – reflecting that current in the country's culture that existed as an alternative to individualism and greed.

In establishing medical facilities, libraries, general assemblies, horizontal grass roots participation in decision-making, in spawning a new communication with "mike-checks," clever hand signals, etc., the occupiers were giving substance to their emerging sense of community. Ultimately, their efforts constituted not only effective protest, but pointed toward a collective ethos, a way of living where cooperation and human solidarity became the foundation for a transformed economic and social order.

## Courage and Persistence

OWS broke through the information barriers to news of rising progressive forces through sheer courage and persistence. The establishment of tent communities populated by people who had been failed by the system could not be ignored. Their willingness to persevere through all kinds of weather, inadequate sanitation, limited diet and in the face of hostility and provocation by the political establishment and police – finally forced the mainstream media to pay attention.

Critically important, OWS was spawned from the ground up. While cooperation and sharing of ideas and actions with unions, civil rights, political action, religious, community and single-issue organizations are vital for building and sustaining the movement, OWS unlike many labor and political organizations did not depend upon top-down direction. Top-down leadership often falters and is drawn away from public battles to attend to its own administrative needs. Perhaps that is one reason why the leadership-directed "One Nation Working Together" effort stumbled while OWS swept across the country – significantly establishing tent communities and political beachheads in cities, big and small and in every region thereby reflecting and representing the country's breadth and social diversity as few dissenting movements have done in the recent past.

The greatest contribution of OWS, widely acknowledged, is to bare the truth of scabrous class inequality. The slogan "we are the 99%" – while technically imprecise, captured as never before the outrageous polarization of wealth and poverty driven by Wall Street– raising the reality of social class and attendant inequality to their rightful place at the top of the domestic agenda. Inseparably tied to that, OWS has stressed the corrosive, corrupting impact of the one percent's money on politics – constituting a brutal and almost unprecedented assault on the country's claims to democracy.

The outcry against inequality and relentless greed did something remarkable. It reduced the dominant public dialogue (or what passes for a dialogue) about the debt (the debt, while serious, is still a relatively small portion of gross domestic product and still not an obstacle to large-scale foreign purchase of US bonds), about cutting social programs, austerity budgets and wrecking already crippled state and local treasuries. Thanks to OWS, inequality and its pervasive social injustice has risen to major concerns in public consciousness. That achievement trumps disingenuous attacks from Fox and the right wing that OWS has not issued demands (actually not true in any case) and from some elements on the left that OWS has allegedly exposed itself to cooptation, and thus betrayal by the Democratic Party and assorted liberal organizations.

## Class Conflict to the Forefront

In bringing class conflict and inequality to the forefront, in demonstrating the effectiveness of demonstrative action, OWS has helped a foundering labor movement recover its collective voice as a foundational instrument of protest and struggle. By delaying often contentious and futile debates about prioritizing corrective measures, instead pounding at the infliction of economic and social pain by Wall Street and the corruption of politics by corporate wealth, OWS has loudly revealed core issues while holding that those in power have the responsibility to find solutions.

Of course, there are legitimate questions regarding the strands of anarchism running through OWS, unwieldy decision-making processes and the need for some coherent democratically evolved leadership. (Those questions need to be advanced modestly by those of us who have been less effective than OWS in movement building).

**Occupy Lexington, Kentucky**

Recent events at Occupy Oakland (California) are particularly ominous and troubling. Faced with a notoriously brutal and racist police department, some elements within Occupy Oakland engaged in provocative and destructive actions, shifting the focus away from the one percent, alienating other participants in the local movement and alienating broader forces so vital for effective, united struggle for economic and social justice. (At this point, it is not known if some of the destruction was fomented by infiltrating provocateurs.) One thing is clear: to allow small groups to act in the name of the Occupy movement is not democracy: it is a negation of democracy. If the movement is to grow and advance, it will have to confront the issues raised by the events in Oakland.

But there is no question that OWS and those groups and individuals that have been drawn to its side take major credit for the rediscovery by a broad public of latent class conflict and class struggle in this country.

Now we have evidence provided by the Pew Research Center that 66% of the public believes that there are "very strong" or strong conflicts

between the rich and poor – an increase of 19% over 2009. Vastly significant is the fact that class conflict ranks ahead of other views of group
conflict and division: immigrants and native born, young and old, blacks
and whites. The perception of class conflict surged "among white people, middle-income earners and independent voters."

The unconscionable shifts in the distribution of wealth have begun to
fray the consciousness of those segments of the population that have
vested heavily in the illusion of upward mobility and a relatively equita-
ble economy. (Forty-three percent continue to believe that the rich made
their fortunes through hard work, ambition and education). Despite illusions, there is fresh potential for healing traditional divisions based on
race, nationality, gender and age and moving towards a relatively unified
working class in defense of its own needs and interests.

## Role of Racism

A reawakening of class conflict is fully consonant with the country's history despite the presence of stubborn conditions that have tended to
undermine class-consciousness essential to class struggle. Racism has
seriously divided the working class and has fostered a false alliance with
the wealthy through the myth of "a white man's country." An advancing
frontier, won largely through genocide committed upon Native Americans, promoted free or cheap land and the belief in upward mobility
as well as belief in "starting over" after initial failures; the availability of
peerless resources and unimpeded access to them, repeated waves of
immigrants to populate an ethnically divided working class – all those
factors, and more, mitigated a coherent, irrepressible class consciousness.

With all that, the United States is perhaps second to none in class struggle (my preferred term). From the first labor stoppages of cordwainers
and other journeymen in the late 18th century, to the strikes of young
women uprooted from the countryside to work in the mills of early 19th
century New England; from the great railroad strike of in 1877; from the
Molly McGuires, the Irish miners who fought the coal barons; from the
Haymarket Martyrs who spurred the great 8-hour-day movement of the
late 19th century; from Eugene Debs' Pullman strike of 1894; from the
Populist wave against oppressive banks and railroads, from the IWW,
the legendary Joe Hill and the Western Federation of Miners who fought
tenaciously against unspeakable employer violence for free speech and
"one big union; from the young men and women of many nationalities
who won the historic Lawrence, Massachusetts "Bread and Roses" strike
(the 100th anniversary of the strike was just celebrated); from the working class opponents of World War I who endured jail sentences; from the
great rail and steel strikes after the war; from the bloody mine struggles

that raged at Blair Mountain in the early twenties to the miners' battles in the Harlan County coal mines; from the San Francisco general strike of 1934 to the auto sit-downs and the upsurge of industrial unionism in the Great Depression; from the anti-fascist mobilization of the work force in World War II to the militant wave of strikes of the early postwar years (that wave suppressed by the union-busting Taft-Hartley Act); to the present-day organizing efforts of Los Angeles janitors and the militant union building and defense of decent health standards by nurses; to the mighty "Wisconsin wave" of tens of thousands of working people who are fighting to save collective bargaining and a decent standard of living and whose actions contributed to an impressive working class mobilization in Ohio that defeated that state's right wing governor's anti-union legislation– all that constitutes a rich history of democratic struggles of working people to claim a rightful share of the wealth that they created.

## Doing the Right Thing

While reciting that list of past struggles, it is important to note that at every critical and potentially transforming juncture in the nation's history, working people did the right thing. After initial hesitation and opposition to unfair draft laws, the working class in the Civil War rallied decisively to the struggle against slavery and for free labor. When conditions in the Great Depression opened the door to massive industrial unionism, the US working class did in five years what it took British labor 100 years to do – it unionized the bulk of basic industries. Millions of workers rallied to the cause of anti-fascism in World War II. In recent years, the working population has increasingly recognized the cost to them (and their sons and daughters) of seemingly endless wars. In the face of manipulated pseudo-patriotic symbolism trotted out at sports events and all kinds of public ceremonies, working people have shown growing restiveness and outright opposition to wars in the Middle East and South Asia.

The working population (literally embracing the 99%) is very different from the core industrial working class of the 1930s and forties. Technological change, corporate globalization, unrelenting anti-labor campaigns by business and government, shifting patterns of immigration driven by global economic change, tilting of the entire economy towards low wage service industries, etc., have altered working class composition where the white industrial worker is no longer the typical representative of the entire class whose composition has been altered by a great influx of women and national minorities. Additionally, the growth of information services has generated large numbers of "professional" computer programmers and other technical workers who indeed are a growing component of the working class.

## Wrong Thinking

A supposition that low-wage service workers are docile, vulnerable and weakly resistant to exploitation – is wrong. Evidence clearly exists that there are new levels of struggle for economic justice by hotel workers, farm workers, immigrants, janitors, hospital and other service employees, public workers, etc. The challenge to the entire 99% is to solidify, deepen and fully support the battle against inequality and against unprecedented corruption of politics by corporate money.

The OWS camps are largely gone for the winter's moment. But OWS' struggle against corporate capital is entering a new stage of concreteness and direct confrontation. Two examples: "move the money" campaigns are growing against the monster banks through efforts to organize withdrawals of accounts from Bank of America, Wells Fargo and other "too big to fail" banks, shifting those funds to credit unions and small community banks. There is growing interest in public banks funded by taxes that would substitute community needs for the institutional greed of mammoth financial enterprises. Echoing the militant mood of the thirties, there are growing movements to resist evictions and to protect victimized homeowners from foreclosures. Among students there is rumbling about a movement to withhold payment of student loans.

The struggle against South African apartheid continues to resonate and supply valuable lessons. Relentless pressure on Polaroid, Chase, Shell Oil, Barclay's and scores of banks and multinational corporations to disinvest in South Africa made the whole apartheid edifice untenable and unsustainable. With nagging economic crisis (there will most likely be cyclical upswings, but the chronic contradictions of the system will not dissolve), we can anticipate that the struggle for economic equality will lead to sharper, more direct confrontations with corporate power – and the political forces that support it.

Success in such efforts mandates the support and participation of the broader progressive community – the unions, the civil rights organizations, the civic and human rights groups, etc. OWS was a catalyst for progressive upsurge. But it cannot be expected to bear the burdens of anti-corporate battle alone. The progressive majority embedded in that wide range of organizations and movements remains a crucial source for a meaningful redirection of the country's political priorities.

At the same time, the currents unleashed by OWS strengthen less transforming but no less essential efforts to beat back the consequences of the current economic crisis. Reemerging militancy is inherent in invigorated movements to close Guantanamo, to stop an assault on Internet speech, to defend reproductive choice, to resist attacks on the right to

vote, to stop the Keystone XL pipeline and anti-environmental legislation, etc.

Ramped up efforts are progressing to push back against the drive of the
one percent and its political acolytes to saddle the 99 percent with the
burdens of "austerity." Countering that pressure are demands to repeal
the Bush tax cuts for the super rich; to put millions to work in building a
green infrastructure, to make the rich pay more for capital gains, to tax
the export of jobs and bring all the troops home.

## Myth of 'Middle class' Society

At the same time, the opportunity and the need for a probing discussion of the nature of capitalism are greater than at any time in recent
memory. Who could have anticipated that the slogan "We are the 99%"
with its contention of grotesque inequality and economic injustice af-
flicting a vast and diverse majority would be embraced by so many of the
public – a public that had been saturated for centuries with the myth of
a "middle class society" of boundless promise?

*CCDS at Fort Benning protest*

It is now widely accepted that Wall Street's insatiable greed and reckless manipulation of the financial system triggered the present economic crisis—the core culprit being risky but highly profitable sub-prime mortgages foisted heavily on the working class and communities of color, then bundled into obscure securities to be sold around the world, poisoning much of the global economy. Dangerous complex instruments like derivatives and credit default swaps generated trillions in escalating losses that sent major investment banks into tailspins. Wall Street received an 800-billion dollar government bailout while those who lost their jobs and homes (for many their only equity) got no help.

The crisis has fallen hardest upon communities of color where institutional racism has pushed unemployment among African Americans to 16.7 percent and to 12 percent among Latinos. In 2009, median household wealth among African Americans was under $6,000 while white household wealth was $113,000—a shocking 20 times greater than financial assets held by blacks.  Racism was a generally unacknowledged factor that drove much of the housing bubble triggering the economic crisis. That underlying factor, fanned by deliberate efforts to foist sub-prime mortgages on communities of color—even upon families that qualified for prime mortgages—was (and remains) systemic—woven deeply into the fabric of capitalism.

## Capitalism is the source

Doubtless, as noted earlier, the unregulated high stakes recklessness of the financial sector brought on the crisis. But capitalism itself is the underlying source of the so-called Great Recession. In a changing political environment that can be attributed in great measure to OWS, it is now possible to gain a hearing on the systemic nature of the present crisis.

Regarding systemic causes, there is the testimony of Nobel Laureate economist Joseph Stiglitz who recently wrote about the fundamental cause of the Great Depression of the 1930s. Stiglitz noted that standard analysis attributes the crisis to a bloated, over-leveraged stock market that crashed on "Black Tuesday" in October 1929. However, he points out that the Depression was gathering force for months before the stock market catastrophe when the substantial farm population was hit by new technologies that led to rapid over production of agricultural commodities, in turn leading to plunging prices and bankruptcies. That led to a collapse of farm purchasing power, to a sharp decline of industrial production and widespread economic collapse. (Stiglitz might have added that signs of coming Depression were grasped by the leading African American newspaper the Pittsburgh Courier more than one year before the general onset of the farm crisis. It warned that black farmers, first to feel the effects of economic crisis, were already experiencing serious contraction in late 1927.)

During the 1970s, the system began to clearly stagnate with the industrial heartland literally rusting. The compulsion within capitalist competition to seek greater production through adding new technologies (while abandoning old processes) accelerated a tendency for the rate of profit to fall (even as the bulk of profit might grow). That falling rate is due to the fact that businesses buy new tools of production—technology (what Marx called constant capital) at full value producing no profit in itself. Profit comes from labor. Marxist theory (now beginning to get an increasingly respectful hearing) posits that the surplus value produced by labor (beyond the actual cost of that labor to the capitalist) is the source of profit realized in sale of the commodity that is produced. But the ratio of fixed capital to labor (variable capital) tends to become inevitably greater. Capitalists attempt to stanch or reverse this process, adding more technology to speed up production and to replace human labor (thus worsening the falling rate of profit) squeezing greater profit through aggressive attacks on wages, through all-out assaults on unions (abetted by their political clout) and most significantly through the globalization of capital—shifting manufacturing to low wage, low tax, countries and regions that are also resistant to unions in what is now widely known as a "race to the bottom."

In the United States, all that has led to a chronic, persistent decline in manufacturing, to disappearing industrial jobs never to return, to unabated wage stagnation and to a gigantic shift to an information and low wage service economy. It has also led to unprecedented aggressiveness by banks and corporations no longer needing to accept New Deal-type reforms for social stability in the face of a declining work force and weakened unions. Those corporations and banks have also aggressively influenced the courts (see Citizens United) and the Congress to deregulate constraints on destructive activities, enact Draconian tax cuts for the super rich, to continue huge military spending (in large measure to shield with arms overseas corporate globalization), consequently adding heavily to the national debt while voicing alarm about that same debt.

## Rule of Finance Capital

Most of all, US capitalism, in abandoning much of domestic manufacturing, is now dominated by the immensely powerful financial sector led by a handful of major investment banks. "Financialization" now virtually governs the economy – producing nothing of substance but feeding upon the lingering assets of the working class and the vast majority of the population. Credit card debt alone is now over $6,000 for every credit cardholder; student loan debt is projected to be over one trillion dollars in 2012. One million three hundred and ninety-five thousand homes are currently in foreclosure.

The housing bubble triggered the crisis, but the underlying cause was the economic weakness and growing impoverishment of the working class and major segments of society. Utilizing impenetrable financial instruments based on such weak economic foundations, Wall Street has been a major source of a global infection—threatening the viability of the European Community and the rest of the world—but also inspiring a search for economic independence and regional cooperation (especially in Latin America and Asia) as a means of escape from the tentacles of global capital.

As the battle to ameliorate the worst effects of the Great Recession grows in the political arena and in the streets, as the fight to tax the rich, to advance an effective stimulus through rebuilding the country's infrastructure and creating millions (not thousands) of new green jobs, through shifting unproductive funds from the military to civilian needs, to reining in the scandalous influence of big money in politics, to fighting resolutely against racism, sexism, homophobia and all forms of division of working people – the question of the nature of crisis-ridden capitalism and a search for creative alternatives will go forward. That too is a consequence of the state of "class warfare" today. Though at times it is difficult to perceive a brighter future in the midst of present-day crises, both history and the present suggest that confidence is fully warranted in working people and their ability to grasp the need for change – and to fight resolutely for it.

*Mark Solomon is a former Co-Chair of CCDS*

# No Stopping Point Short of Victory:

## Interviewing Michelle Crentsil
## on Race, Class and Occupy!

### By Pat Fry

It didn't take long for Michelle Crentsil to grab her friend and make way down to Zuccotti Park for the occupation of Wall Street last September. From day two, Michelle and her friend were there, two of the few African Americans who began giving shape and voice to the 99% movement.

"We were approached and interviewed by so many in the media asking us about our involvement in OWS," said Michelle, "because there was such a dearth of people of color." Sitting down to share her experience with this writer Michelle explained that the reason why there were so few was evident in the General Assembly discussions of the first OWS declaration.

*Michelle Crentsil*

"There were tensions and misunderstandings about the role of race and racism," explained Michelle. The dominant view was that "we are all people, we are all the same." That struck a sour chord with Michelle and other activists who formed the OWS People of Color Working Group. "We are not all the same. We cannot erase the history of racism in this country. Race is central to everything and it is important to see how class, race and gender intersect. A lot of us are facing serious issues of racialized marginalization and we can't just erase that."

The rift grew over this issue, Michelle explained. "When it was raised in the General Assembly it was a noticeably tense moment—you had the feeling that some felt that we were just being mean. In fact, some folks actually said that. It showed the depth of the misunderstanding about how race is central to any analysis we are talking about. Racism isn't extraneous—it is a pillar of capitalism. You can't separate race and class in this country."

For Michelle, an important university history class entitled Slavery, Capitalism and Imperialism "really opened my eyes, making the historical connections between racism and its central role in the development of capitalism."

"The whole idea that we had to create a People of Color working group" speaks for itself, said Michelle. "It is now named the People of Color Caucus but we call it POCCUPY for short," she said.

"If we are addressing capitalism as a problem we are central, not marginal. The movement against capitalism has to be led by people of color. And, it won't happen unless there are intentional and deliberate steps taken to bring this about. That was the impetus behind forming our People of Color group."

This led to the organizing of one of the most successful workshops of the OWS movement. Michelle and others of POCCUPY along with an Anti-Racism Allies Group sponsored the "Organizing through a Racial Justice Framework" workshop. Working with Color Lines and the Applied Research Center, the workshop looked at institutional racism, how it manifests itself as an obstacle to organizing, and providing a tool kit of ways to take it on.

## Racism is a Pillar of Capitalism

"That's what the workshop was about—racism as a pillar of capitalism," said Michelle. Drawing from the experience of an organizing model among immigrant workers in New York City restaurants, Michelle said the strategy utilizes the concept of organizing from the margins to the center. The campaign of the Restaurant Opportunity Center begins with reaching workers in the kitchens first and pushing to the center of the restaurant organizing campaigns. "Building power at the margins is a requirement if we want to build power for society as a whole," said Michelle.

The turnout for the workshop went way beyond expectations. "We thought maybe 50 people would show up and we were really worried it would not succeed," said Michelle. "But nearly 400 people came—we were blown away."

People participated from many different walks of life—from social workers to activists representing community organizations and from throughout the state. Syracuse and Albany occupy movements came. "Racially, it was probably the most diverse event I have seen in a very long time," said Michelle. Many of the working groups of OWS came as well – from the Labor Outreach, movement building, direct action and others. "This is exactly what we wanted. We wanted everyone in the room."

One of the reasons for the high turnout, said Michelle, was that people were eager to discuss how to deal with racism. "There were a lot of interpersonal issues—instances of racism at OWS," said Michelle. "People have the idea that because this is a progressive, radical movement, we didn't have these problems. People became paralyzed by it. We would have meetings using a consensus process and talk about how everyone has a voice—but it was the same non-marginalized people doing the talking—white men speaking for the undocumented or Black or Latino communities—but the people they were talking about were not in the room. So we asked, why not?"

The workshop was organized to deal with these issues on the spot and to work through the problems in order to move forward. "We have to push each other—and we have to agree to push each other. This is what I said in my opening remarks," said Michelle. "Expect to be pushed because this is the only way we can make change. We have to talk about who's not in the room and why, instead of not wanting to talk about it. This means organizing through a racial justice framework."

## 'How Can We Move Our Own People'

Following the workshop, there was a meeting called on short notice to debrief and surprisingly, said Michelle, 50 people attended. "It was impressive and wonderful because a lot of different people attended." Activists from the South Bronx Latino community came and said they appreciated the workshop. They made the point that they don't need people from OWS to come to the South Bronx but wanted to learn the strategies on organizing for their own community. "This is exactly what we wanted to achieve," said Michelle. "How can we move our own people, our own communities? We want to start the movement in our communities and that's what we accomplished with the workshop," she said.

"We want this to keep continuing. We felt terrible about the negative things in the beginning of the Occupy days—there was no understanding of the importance of a racial justice framework and what it means to not want to talk about it. We cannot ignore it." For Michelle and others it was a question of whether they would stay involved in the occupy movement.

Other trainings have spun off from the workshop, said Michelle. Anti-oppression trainings are taking place organized by sub groups of OWS groups, she said. There is the People of Color Direct Action, a sub group of Direct Action and POCCUPY which is open to all people, not only people of color. They work closely with the Take Back the Bronx group. "This is a big change from the beginnings of the occupy movement," said Michelle.

"Winter has been a big test for people because of the cold but it has also been a good time for building and talking about who is missing, what needs to be done to change it, and talking about who are not in the fore-front of OWS," she continued.

## Organization Is Critical

In the build up for May Day actions this year, Michelle said it will be a display of our power but it will take organizing, using the tools learned from the workshop. "In Flatbush, for example, if people decided to open a communal breakfast program, or work to build a new playground or-ganizing in a community bound together as a constituency—this is what should take place not because Occupy decides but what the community decides and Occupy supporting it," said Michelle.

A second workshop is in the works. The title has not yet been decided but it will focus on labor in NYC through a racial justice framework. "The panel will be representive of the demographics of the working people of the city, and it will hammer home the idea that you cannot separate race and class. When we talk about income inequality, we have to talk about race," said Michelle. Plans are to draw from the experiences of recent la-bor battles—the Transport Workers Union contract fight, the Teamster's Sotheby union-busting lock out, and the CWA Cablevision organizing victory—struggles of largely African American and Latino workers.

In honor of Dr. Martin Luther King Day in January, a large rally was held in front of Madison Square Garden in Manhattan. Along with many com-munity organizers, labor and elected officials, Michelle spoke as an OWS and People of Color activist. The Knicks were playing at the same time inside the stadium where the CWA Cablevision workers had unfurled a huge banner from the rafters during half-time that read: Cablevision 99% - CWA. Two busloads of Cablevision workers attended the rally outside a few days before the union election for CWA representation.

Inspired and moved, Michelle's message that day to the crowd was about the importance of continuing the work of Dr. King's commitment to ra-cial and economic justice. "They are tied together and that is why he did so much work for the labor movement."

"Dr. King said there is no stopping point short of victory," said Michelle addressing the rally. "Victory is when the Cablevision workers and all workers can retire with pensions. Victory is when we all have a union as a right. Victory is when Black workers don't make less than white workers. There is no stopping point short of victory and we won't stop until we win."

*Pat Fry is a trade unionist, labor writer and a national co-chair of the Committees of Correspondence for Democracy and Socialism*

# From 'Planton' to Occupy:
# Unions and Immigrants
# and the Occupy Movement

### *By David Bacon*

When Occupy Seattle called its tent camp "Planton Seattle," organizers were laying a local claim to a set of tactics used for decades by social

movements in Mexico, Central America and the Philippines. And when immigrant janitors marched down to the detention center in San Diego and called their effort Occupy ICE (the initials of the Immigration and Custom Enforcement agency responsible for mass deportations), people from countries with that planton tradition were connecting it to the Occupy movement here.

This shared culture and history offer new possibilities to the Occupy movement for survival and growth at a time when the Federal law enforcement establishment, in cooperation with local police departments and municipal governments, has uprooted many tent encampments. Different Occupy groups from Wall Street to San Francisco have begun to explore their relationship with immigrant social movements in the U.S., and to look more closely at the actions of the 1% beyond our borders that produces much of the pressure for migration.

Reacting to the recent evictions, the Coalition for the Political Rights of Mexicans Abroad recently sent a support letter to Occupy Wall Street and the other camps under attack. "We greet your movement," it declared, "because your struggle against the suppression of human rights and against social and economic injustice has been a fundamental part of our struggle, that of the Mexican people who cross borders, and the millions of Mexican migrants who live in the United States."

Many of those migrants living in the U.S. know the tradition of the planton and how it's used at home. And they know that the 1%, whose power is being challenged on Wall Street, also designed the policies that are the very reason why immigrants are living in the U.S. to begin with. Mike Garcia, president of United Service Workers West/SEIU, the union that organized Occupy ICE, described immigrant janitors as "displaced workers of the new global economic order, an order led by the West and the United States in particular."

Criminalizing the act of camping out in a public space is intended, at least in part, to keep a planton tradition from acquiring the same legitimacy in the U.S. that it has in other countries. That right to a planton was not freely conceded by the rulers of Mexico, El Salvador or the Philippines, however—no more than it has been conceded here. The 99% of those countries had to fight for it.

Two of the biggest battles of modern Mexican political history were fought in the Tlatelolco Plaza, where hundreds of students were gunned down in 1968, and three years later in Mexico City streets where more were beaten and shot by the paramilitary Halcones. In both El Salvador and the Philippines, strikers have a tradition of living at the gates of the factory or enterprise where they work. But even today that right must be defended against the police, and (at least until the recent election of the Funes and Aquino governments) even the military.

Plantons or encampments don't stand alone. They are tactics used by unions, students, farmers, indigenous organizations and other social movements. Each planton is a visible piece of a movement or organization—a much larger base. When the plantons are useful to those movements, they defend them. That connection between planton and movement, between the encampment and its social base, is as important as holding the physical space on which the tents are erected.

For the last two years that relationship has been very clear in the Zocalo, Mexico City's huge central plaza. During that time, fired members of Mexico's independent leftwing electrical workers union, the SME, have lived in a succession of plantons. They've often been elaborate, with kitchens, meeting rooms and communications centers, in addition to the tents where people slept and ate.

At various time, the SME encampment was one of several in the huge square. A year ago the workers were joined by indigenous Triqui and Mixtec women from Oaxaca, who protested the violence used by their state's previous governor against teachers' strikes and rural organizations. The social movement in Oaxaca, which the women represented in Mexico City, grew strong enough to finally knock the old ruling party, the PRI, from the governorship it had held for almost 80 years.

In the Zocalo plantons, people from different organizations mix it up. Last September's Day of the Indignant brought together people from very diverse movements.  Some see electoral politics as a vehicle for change, but many indigenous activists and SME members don't.  Even among those who do, there are deep disagreements over how to partici-pate in the electoral process.

## The Planton as a Magnet for Attention

But the people in the Zocalo have two things in common.  Different plan-tons may not see every political question eye-to-eye, but each represents a social movement in the world outside the plaza.  And the planton itself has value primarily because it forces public attention to focus on the crisis that has led each group to set up its encampment.

The SME workers used their plantons to dramatize repression by the Federal government. When Mexican President Felipe Calderon dissolved the state-run power company for central Mexico and fired its 44,000 em-ployees, he sought to destroy their union and move towards the privati-zation of the electrical system -- to benefit Mexican and foreign 1%ers. A year ago, several SME members conducted a hunger strike at the planton that generated front page headlines for weeks, and lasted so long that doctors warned participants they were risking death.  At the height of the protest, the union battled police in front of the power stations, as it tried to exercise its legal right to strike and picket.

The planton and the movement outside it were intimately connected. The hunger strikers were few, but spoke for a union of tens of thou-sands of workers. In the end, the SME negotiated the removal of its last planton in return for government acknowledgement of its right to exist. It organized other unions to resist the government's assault on labor rights, and mobilized electricity consumers to protest rising bills and cuts in service. The planton helped to focus attention on these demands, and to pull the union's allies into action.

## Fertilization Across Borders

Clearly someone in Seattle knows this tradition of plantons in the Zo-calo, perhaps even as a participant. When the painter made the Seattle banner, she or he also included, right next to the word "planton", the anarchists' "A" with the circle around it. This symbol was a reminder of another aspect of cross-border fertilization. Many anarchists or anarcho-syndicalists—members of the Industrial Workers of the World—fought in the Mexican Revolution. Because of that revolutionary upheaval, even today, almost a century later, ordinary Mexicans expect certain rights, including the right to set up a tent in the Zocalo. U.S. workers crossed

the border to fight alongside Mexicans in that insurrection long ago, for a government that would acknowledge that right. The planton, therefore, is a common heritage, with a history that makes it as legitimate on Wall Street as it is in Mexico City.

Not long after the OWS camp was set up in Zuccotti Park, the planton/occupy movement crossed the U.S./Mexico border. In Tijuana, home to a million people, mostly displaced migrants from Mexico's south, activists came together and set up an occupation on the grassy median of the Paseo de los Heroes. Their tents were pitched in the middle of the Zona del Rio, where the city's 1% meet in fancy hotels and work in government offices. Then, on October 18 police reacted even earlier than they did in most U.S. cities, arresting two dozen activists at the urging of local businessmen. Occupy Tijuana condemned the detentions, declaring, "We are not assassins, delinquents, tramps or crooks."

In the U.S. we have our own history of defending public space for protest, and it isn't necessary to reach back a hundred years to find it. In just the last few decades, immigrant workers have popularized the use of the planton here, helping unions recover the militant tactics of their own past. In 1992 immigrants trying to join the United Electrical Workers mounted the first strike among production workers in Silicon Valley, and set up a planton and conducted a hunger strike to pressure their employer. A year later other Latino immigrants in San Francisco erected their tents on the sidewalk in front of Sprint's headquarters, after their workplace was closed days before they were scheduled to vote in a union election.

## WTO Protests in Seattle

A decade ago anti-globalization activists and unions shut down the meeting of the World Trade Organization in Seattle. Young protestors chained their arms together inside metal pipes, and lay down in the intersections of downtown Seattle. Tens of thousands took over the streets. Other anti-globalization protests followed, in which activists battled for their right to use public space to challenge the international policies of the 1%.

Working-class support for the battle in Seattle had its roots in the impact of the North American Free Trade Agreement. Workers could see the cost of free trade in the loss of their own jobs, as production moved south. Over the last two decades, many have also discovered that those same agreements and policies didn't make Mexicans better off, but led to their impoverishment as well.

NAFTA and free market policies forced on developing countries produced opportunities for banks and corporations to reap profits. They drove down wages, forced farmers off their land, and destroyed the unions and livelihood of millions of people. This system was designed on Wall Street, by the same bankers Occupiers hold responsible for the current crisis of foreclosures and unemployment in the U.S. The current economic crisis doesn't stop at the border. In fact in Mexico, Central America, the Philippines and elsewhere, it's been a fact of life for a long time. This is the source of forced migration—what Garcia condemned at Occupy ICE.

The 99% live in all those countries where free trade agreements and structural adjustment policies are imposed. They also live in the communities of people who have come here as a result. Who, then, are more natural allies for Occupy protestors than people who've been on the receiving end of these policies for years?

In New York this connection wasn't lost on Occupy Wall Street. In October a group, Occupy Wall Street-Español was formed at the first Asemblea en Español. They, in turn, translated the first issue of the Occupied Wall Street Journal. Participants formed a subgroup, Occupy Wall Street Latinoamericano to spread the movement to Spanish-speaking communities, recognizing that the city is home to so many Mexicans from the state of Puebla that its nickname is PueblaYork, as well as much older established communities of Puerto Ricans, Colombians, Ecuadorians and other Spanish-speaking people. The group will soon publish the first

issue of its own newspaper, with articles talking about immigration, globalization, and the specific attacks by the 1% on Latinos.

Claudia Villegas, a women's rights activist working with the group Occupy Wall Street Latinoamericano, helped organize a demonstration of
immigrant women four days after police raided the Zuccotti Park encampment. "We decided to change our original plan for a march because
we were afraid they would stop it," she says. "Nevertheless, 23 organizations participated including women's rights groups and above all, those
working with immigrant women."

## United Action in San Francisco

In San Francisco a joint march of immigrant activists and Occupy participants helped to defend that city's encampment. In the general assembly
meeting preceding it participants talked about the city's offer to move
the Occupiers into an abandoned building in the Latino Mission District
several miles away. Few wanted to give up the camp on Justin Herman
Plaza, and most felt the city was just trying to move them out of sight.
But many people also felt that having an Occupy camp in the barrio was
a good idea.

"We're still really working in parallel," Villegas says. She draws attention
to the potential power of the immigrant rights movement, and what it
could mean to OWS. "We have to include the movement that began in
2006, when there were hundreds of thousands of people in the streets
across this country. eople were reacting to the injustice of the system
then too." They're separate movements, though, she warns, and "our
agenda has to come from immigrants themselves. We need to integrate,
and at the same time the Occupy movement has to learn to accept us.
But we're all on the same path."

Bringing the immigrant and Occupy movements together means more
than setting up an encampment. The San Diego demonstration didn't set
up an overnight camp, but it brought thousands of workers and supporters down to the ICE detention center to protest the firings of immigrant
janitors.

The Occupy ICE protest was intended to draw public attention to the
Federal government's immigration enforcement strategy that requires
employers to fire undocumented workers. In Southern California, the
multinational corporations who clean office buildings are terminating
2000 union members. Earlier waves of firings have targeted unionized
building cleaners in Minneapolis, Seattle and San Francisco, sewing machine operators in Los Angeles, food service workers on university cam-
puses, and thousands of others.

Garcia says ICE and the employers are in collusion. After firing union janitors with high seniority and benefits, using immigration status as a pretext, the companies can then hire new workers at lower wages with fewer benefits. "To hide their greed the commercial real estate industry has used the tools of government to confuse and divide the 99%," he charges. "They first said we were unskilled workers who should be happy to be working. They then weakened worker protections to make organizing virtually impossible. Over the last decade the industry has used immigration as a wedge to intimidate and, if need be, replace our workers. ICE is doing what the 1% corporate real estate industry wants: using immigration laws to recycle well paid janitors in the hopes of taking back gains in pay and benefits our union has won." [Ironically the week USWW organized Occupy ICE its parent union, SEIU, endorsed the reelection of President Obama, who is responsible for the ICE policy of firing workers.]

## Importance of Worker Defense

For Occupy, defending workers under attack is a way to survive, grow roots and develop a strong base. That's not always the direction activists take, however. Near Oakland, over two hundred immigrant workers at the largest foundry on the west coast, Pacific Steel Casting in Berkeley, are being fired in another "silent raid" like that hitting the janitors. Through the summer and fall, foundry workers went to city councils, unions, churches and community organizations, seeking help to pressure ICE not to force them from their jobs. Their campaign held "the migra" off for months, but the firings began nevertheless in November. Now these immigrant families are trying to survive. It is important for Occupy Oakland to respond to the crisis of these workers. And beyond the Bay Area, Occupy movements could develop much stronger relationships with immigrant communities if they helped workers fight against immigration-related firings and detentions. OWS has yet to respond, however.

Solidarity is a two-way street, based on mutual respect. In most cities, including Oakland and San Francisco, labor has welcomed Occupy and sought to defend the encampments. In New York, Occupy activists have been given resources in many union halls, and unions have mobilized against police raids at Zuccotti Park. An alliance of unions, immigrants and Occupiers has great potential strength, not just in numbers, but also in the exchange of ideas and tactics. Unions in particular might benefit from wider use of the planton or Occupy encampment. Occupy ICE challenges the Occupy movement to take up the firings of immigrant workers, but it's also a challenge to unions themselves, many of whom have watched in silence as longtime members were forced from their jobs.

The vision of Occupy—the 99% vs. the 1%—has enormous support among immigrants and unions. In place of the tired rhetoric of politicians, shedding crocodile tears for the "middle class" while demonizing the poor, Occupy gives workers a vision of their commonality in the 99%. This powerful message blows away illusions that higher-paid workers have more in common with stockbrokers than with immigrants laboring at minimum wage, or unemployed young people on the streets of African American ghettos or Latino barrios.

The Coalition for the Political Rights of Mexicans Abroad shares the same vision of class-based commonality. "We are outraged," it says, "that U.S. citizens, when they demand justice and expose the inequalities that exist in their society, are treated like criminals. With the same outrage, we condemn the criminalization of migrant Mexicans by the U.S. government, the raids by immigration authorities [and] the militarization of the border...No human being should be treated as a criminal because they struggle to find better conditions in which to live."

*David Bacon is a writer and photojournalist widely known for documenting the connections between labor, migration, and the global economy*

# Labor Message to Occupy: Stop Republicans from Turning Back the Clock On Civil Rights

## By Ken Riley

Good evening, everyone. I would like to take this opportunity to welcome each of you to our home, the headquarters of the International

Longshoremen Association, ILA Local 1422. The movie industry is alive and well here in Charleston. If it wasn't for the filming of Army Wives tomorrow, this event would have been held down in the community hall.

Therefore I must issue a warning here this evening. You are currently seated in our hiring hall. If we receive a request for labor this evening, we are bound by law to hire from the individuals who are present in the hiring hall. So while you all are out there looking so pretty and dressed up, I hope you have your coveralls, hard hats, gloves, and steel toe shoes in your automobiles, because, you will have to go to work. A refusal could result in a 7, 14, or 30 day suspension.

### Remembering Dr. King

Nevertheless, I believe it is fitting that we find ourselves here tonight, not in a decorated auditorium but in a place where working men and women assemble everyday to seek work, and to provide a decent living for their families. I believe it is only fitting that we find ourselves in a Union Hall, yes a Union Hall, in South Carolina, as we commemorate the legacy of the Rev. Dr. Martin Luther King, a legacy which included the struggle for dignity in the workplace. Even Dr. King realized that the best way to secure fair wages, safe working conditions, healthcare, pensions, and most of all respect in the workplace, was by organizing.

That is why he went to Memphis. That is why he died. He recognized that workers rights are civil rights. He realized that these rights would

*Transit Workers Back OWS in New York City*

be more secured within a union. As Dr. King traveled throughout this country and throughout the south in particular, he witnessed firsthand the calamities associated with an ever intensifying class war. He warned us, in Memphis, in 1968. While addressing the Poor People's Campaign, Dr. King made this point, "We have developed an underclass in this nation. And unless this underclass is made a working class, we are going to continue to have problems."

Brothers and sisters we have major problems in this country which are continuing and growing. Why? Because for the first time in a long time, we are witnessing the disappearance of the middle class and its foundation, which is organized labor. It was the unions that built the middle class in America and in particular the black middle class.

So now, the corporate barons, the right wing conservatives, and the Republican Party have declared war on the middle class and as you can plainly see, they in are in full battle mode. They are turning back the clock. In my opinion, their primary target is organized labor, the Unions. Why, because of the amount of damage that can be done by eliminating them.

Eliminate the unions and corporate profits will soar, all on the backs of the working poor.

Eliminate the unions and the middle class will crumble.

Eliminate the unions and a major source of funding for the Democratic Party or any other socially conscious party will evaporate.

Eliminate the unions and the only true voice of working people will be silenced.

Eliminate the unions and many benefits that you as workers currently enjoy, whether you are union or not, will begin to disintegrate.

Remember, make no mistake about it. It was the unions that brought you: the 40 hour work week; the weekend; paid holidays and vacations; employer-provided healthcare; pensions; sick leave; Family Medical Leave Act; Minimum Wage laws; OSHA; the NLRB.

Corporate America, foreign capital, and the Republican Party have declared war on the working people of our communities, where some have accepted it and internalized it.

But most importantly let us prepare quickly to defend against it. If this is war, then we must act as though it is a war. Working people in Wisconsin and Ohio understand that this is war. Occupy Wall Street, Occupy Oakland, and Occupy Charleston and yes Occupiers all over this nation understand that this is war. The longshoremen up in Longview, Washington who are preparing for a major fight this month understand what this is all about.

Listen, we are not going to let them turn back the clock. We are not going to let them. The Republicans are campaigning here in South Carolina this week on the theme that they are going to take back America. How in the world you are going to take back something you already have taken? No, we the people are going to take back America, beginning in November when we re-elect Barrack Obama, President of the United States of America.

Again, Welcome to the House of Labor in this community, the headquarters of the International Longshoremen Association, ILA Local 1422. Please enjoy the evening.

**Ken Riley is president of the International Longshoremen's Association Local 1422 in South Carolina**

# 2012: A Year for Making Demands and Building Even Bigger Protests

## *By Paul Krehbiel*

What a difference a year makes. At the beginning of 2011, the national debate—at least the discussion the mainstream corporate media and political leaders were having—was about huge budget deficits and making devastating cutbacks in our vital social services. And the public was relatively quiet.

As the year progressed millions of people, including growing numbers in the power elite, demanded a stop to the cuts, restoring crippled programs, the creation of millions of jobs, affordable health care and education, stopping the right-wing juggernaut, and making the top 1% and their corporations pay their fair share. Massive demonstrations, marches, occupations and other protests marked the past year. As we begin 2012 we need more of the same, but bigger.

The large protests began in February 2011 in Wisconsin when tens of thousands of unionized public workers and their allies staged massive demonstrations and an occupation of their state capitol to protest right-wing Republican Governor Scott Walker's move to strip public workers of their collective bargaining rights and destroy their unions. Union-led movements sprang up in Ohio, New Jersey and other states where right-wing governors tried the same thing, which in turn sparked nation-wide demonstrations by union workers in every state.

### Student and Youth

Students followed with huge demonstrations against skyrocketing tuitions, and people of color and immigrants marched against discrimination and for full civil rights. In September in New York City, a new movement connected all the dots and occupied Wall Street with a tent city. The Occupy movement swept the country for the rest of the year demanding that the top 1% stop fleecing the 99%. As 2012 begins, the national discourse must now include ideas on how to raise the money to pay for all the things the 99% need.

Voices in all of these movements say the problem has been a decades-long shifting of money out of the pockets of the 99% and into the pockets of the top 1%, resulting in the greatest transfer of wealth in the history of our country. There is enough money to fund every program, create millions of jobs, and provide high quality, affordable health care and education for all. How did we get in this mess, and how can we get out?

For one thing the tax structure is completely out of whack. The people who have siphoned off the most from the system are too often paying the least, or nothing, or even getting rebates from what the rest of us pay. After WWII, corporations paid over 40% of all federal taxes. Today, corporations pay less than 10%, and even lower in most states. There is no way the rest of us, the 99%, can make up the difference.

Average pay for US wage and salary workers is about $40,000 a year, less when adjusted for inflation. Top executives of the largest 299 corporations averaged $11.4 million in income in 2010 (figures for 2011 aren't available as of this writing), according to the AFL-CIO, the major national federation of unions. This 13-million member union body supports raising the taxes on the top 1% and their corporations and banks and shifting money to social needs and the creation of jobs. The money is there. Tons of it. The rich are just sitting on it. According to Moody's, the financial analyst, 1,600 US-based corporations were holding $1.2 trillion in cash at the end of 2010, and not investing it in more production, services or US jobs (numbers for 2011 aren't out yet but its more of the same.) Many of these giant corporations and banks reported record profits, while millions of people sink into poverty.

## Reforms Worth Fighting For

How to fix this: Close tax loopholes for the very wealthy and their corporations and banks, and increase their tax rates. Also, end their offshore tax havens, and assess a tax on all financial transactions (the California Nurses Association has a campaign on this.) From the end of WWII until the 1960's, the top income tax rate for the very rich—the 1%, was 90%. Today its 35%, but most pay much less. Congress could make these changes and raise hundreds of billions of dollars.

But Congress won't do this on its own—they rely on big contributions from the 1% to get elected and stay in office. The only solution is to build a bigger mass movement. It must be on the scale of the power-

**Youth Workshop at CCDS Convention, 2009**

ful movement of workers in the 1930's-40's that built huge unions and which won Social Security, unemployment insurance and other economic social safety net programs. It must be on the scale of the movements of the 1960's for civil rights, against the war in Vietnam, for student's and women's rights, and for new freedoms for everyone.

Since most of our armed forces came home at the end of 2011, we have a great opportunity today to demand that the huge amounts of money from the war in Iraq be used to fund social needs. Consider this. In 2011, 42 states, including California, had a combined deficit of $105 billion. The wars in Iraq, Afghanistan, and Pakistan for 2011 cost $159 billion. If we had brought all our troops and military contractors home at the beginning of 2011, the savings could have funded every state deficit, restored every cut program, and kept hundreds of thousands of public workers who lost their jobs, employed. A number of organizations are working to transfer money from the war to social needs, including US Labor Against the War, Code Pink, and other anti-war and community organizations, and this demand has been raised at Occupy protests and others. But we must ratchet up the protests for the transfer of money from the military to social needs.

Jobs have been the public's number one concern since the 2007-08 recession. Yet, the private sector hasn't reduced unemployment one iota while 20 million people want to work. While many economists have called our four-year economic crisis a "recession," for the unemployed it's been a depression. Let's re-establish an expanded Works Progress Administration, begun by President Roosevelt in 1935 in the Great Depression, which gave 8 million people jobs. We need people today to rebuild crumbling roads, bridges, schools and hospitals. That would put people back to work making improvements that we need as a society, and get paychecks into the hands of people who will spend it in hard-pressed local economies all across the country. The AFL-CIO and other organizations are working for a massive jobs creation program. We must add our voices to this demand.

Some politicians and their wealthy corporate backers are still pushing to cut Medicare, Social Security and Medicaid, lifelines for millions, to supposedly balance our budget. That proposal goes in exactly the opposite direction of where we should be going. Rather than cutbacks, let's broaden Medicare to cover everyone. Our non-profit government-financed Medicare, Social Security and Medicaid programs have administrative costs of just 3%-5%, while the private, for-profit health insurance companies take 25%-27% for administrative costs (which go for high executive salaries, dividends to stockholders, and advertising).

## Medicare for All

Establishing a Medicare-for-All health care system would stop the health insurance industry from stuffing $400 billion of our health premium dollars into their bank accounts, and allow that money to be used to provide quality health care services for all. Here in California a number of organizations are promoting this type of program, including Health Care for All and many unions, senior organizations, and community groups. Contact an organization that is working for these programs and offer to lend a hand and help them build the broad political movements needed to make them a reality. 2012 should look like 2011, but bigger.

*Paul Krehbiel is a CCDS member, writer and labor organizer in the Los Angeles area*

# Occupy Lexington:
# 100+ days and still counting!
# A Personal Reflection

*By Janet Tucker*

On January 7, 2012, Occupy Lexington celebrated our 100th day. What a rich experience this has been! This amazing movement, which was sparked by the Arab Spring and the events in Wisconsin, has spread like wildfire across the country and around the world.

Here in Lexington, Kentucky our Occupy camped out in front of Chase Bank on Main Street. We are one of the smaller Occupies for sure, but no less amazing. Starting out on September 29, just 9 days after Occupy Wall Street, we now claim to be the longest running continuous occupation in the US. We have been there so long that the postal service has delivered us mail addressed to "Occupy Lexington"!

I have met so many wonderful activists and have made many new friends. We have come to consider ourselves family in many ways. While there have been people of all ages, there is a solid group of young people, with their tremendous stamina, keeping this thing going, staying out in the cold, rain, and snow. They stay there because they have a desire to help create a better world.

We have gotten good support from the community, from honks from passing motorists to donations of food, supplies and money. People stop by on a regular basis to talk, if not in support, then just to ask questions, wanting to know who we are and why we are there. We have been given publishing space in a local community paper and have developed a newsletter to expand our outreach to the community.

While our numbers have dwindled some since the beginning, the activities have increased. Most of the occupiers are under-employed or unemployed workers. The back bone of this occupation has been working class young people with students from the University of Kentucky playing a supportive role.

General Assemblies are a daily occurrence, just as they are elsewhere. These are an important area for education and discussion. After some disputes, the group came to the conclusion that conflicts of an interpersonal character needed to be handled elsewhere. Occupy Lexington realized that they must spend their time on why they came together in the first place—the plight of the 99%. By refocusing attention on the main tasks, solidarity and morale has improved.

Actions, teach-ins, and working groups are regular occurrences. We have had "mic checks" at Walmart and at foreclosure auctions. We've had marches and rallies including a rally on December 10 in support of voting rights. We worked with the local Move to Amend group to plan an "Occupy the Courts" on January 20.Volunteering with local organizations is one way we have reached into the greater community. For example, we distributed flyers for the Rescue Mission to publicize their free Thanksgiving dinner and we did a food and toy drive leading up to the holidays. Occu-parties are a regular occurrence on Saturday nights.

We have rallied in support of our state Senator, Kathy Stein. She is an outstanding legislator who has always stood on the right side of issues and has never been afraid to speak her mind. She is a supporter of our occupation and has visited regularly with various donations and just to talk. State Senate Republicans basically fired her through redistricting. While many of us were at a rally against this redistricting in our state capital, the Lexington police raided our encampment and tore down all of our tents. We have nevertheless maintained the occupation with these glorious young people working in shifts to stay there even without the tents. Whether we continue to "occupy" through the winter still remains to be seen. The physical occupation has to be seen as a tactic in a broad array of tactics available to this movement. Regardless, the Occupy Movement will continue. And American spring is coming!

## Inspiring Other Campaigns

Through Occupy Lexington other important mobilizations have emerged. For example, along with the national "move your money" campaign urging people to move their money out of big banks, we have "Invest in Kentucky". This campaign calls on our state treasury to move state funds that currently are in Chase Bank to local banks or credit unions. We have initiated an on-line petition campaign which anyone can sign by going to investinky.org.

Another work group is the "People's Budget," which partially grew out of the movement to support Lexington city workers as they rallied against increased health insurance costs. Presently we are studying the 576-page city budget, meeting and talking with city workers from different

***Workshop on Media in Lexington***

departments, with folks in the community, and engaging more with the City Council by going to their various meetings and working sessions. This is no small project by any means but we hope to be ready to engage in further discussions when the Council begins to discuss the new budget this spring so it can better serve the pople of Lexington.

Occupy Lexington needs to do more outreach to other organizations in the city on both of these campaigns as it will take a much broader movement for them to be successful. We have participated in the events of other organizations and some members from those groups come down to the Occupy site and participate in our events. And it is also important to bring new folks into these mass organizations.

## Learning from Each Other

There are many people in these organizations who have been involved in struggle for many years and have much to teach new people coming in. At the same time these new people bring new energy and vitality and new ideas to these organizations. Bringing them into an organization will necessarily change that organization! I have heard so often from many of the organization I have been involved in: "We need young people", "Where are the young people?" "How can we get young people involved?" Well I want to say loud and clear "Here they are!" And all the traditional progressive organizations should be prepared to welcome occupiers and engage in mutual learning.

In addition, building organization is an important task. In cities where the occupations have been brutally shut down by the police, organization continues, particularly General Assemblies and working groups. Plans are already under way for the spring.

Along with doing outreach to other progressive organizations, it is vitally for the occupy movement to build strong unity with the broader working class movement, the trade unions and the African American and other national minority movements for justice. These are at the core of the progressive majority. Only with this strategic alliance can the struggle of the 99% make significant advances. So far in Lexington, we have had some people of color spend time at the occupy movement but the sustaining participants are mostly white. We have gotten verbal support from organized labor but not much activism. These patterns raise challenges for us in Lexington.

While building mass organizations, it is also important to connect people to socialist organizations such as CCDS. To do this it is necessary to build relationships and trust and to do revolutionary education. Occupiers have been invited to participate in our meetings of "CCDS and Friends."

Also teach-ins and education have been a regular part of the occupation. We have had film showings and a live performance such as "Marx in Soho," several ongoing study groups including a book study on corporate personhood. But education is a two way street. Teachers are learners and learners are teachers. I have learned much from my new friends both young and old but mostly young.

The world is a difficult place for young adults today, with no jobs, horrific student loans and debts, no health care coverage. And they are motivated by righteous anger against this. As one occupier told me "This is what I have been waiting for my whole life!" And they have a quest for knowledge!

Furthermore, this is really the first time I have had personal relationships with people who are homeless on any scale. These people are shunned and ignored. They are those that our city does not want to acknowledge. They are all living on the street for different reasons but their daily struggle just to survive should humble us all.

Aside from participating in the educational activities on site, our local "CCDS and Friends" has started working with the University of Kentucky Socialist Student Union and other socialists in the area and has developed a Socialist Study Group. While our educational activities are separate from the occupiers, we support them, and as individuals many of us are a part of Occupy Lexington. Recently two members of Occupy Boston, Rafael and Alex, visited Occupy Lexington and local members of "CCDS and Friends." We had a very rich discussion of the occupation both now and in the future and the role of socialists in this movement.

It has been amazing to be involved in what is a small part of this national and international uprising. The key tasks facing Occupy are to build lasting organization, do education, and unite with labor and oppressed nationalities and other groups and organizations forming a progressive majority that is truly representative of the 99%.

*Janet Tucker is a veteran organizer in Lexington, Kentucky, and the National Coordinator of CCDS*

# Some Thoughts on Occupy Boston from a Peace Movement Perspective

## By Duncan McFarland

"How to fix the deficit? End the wars and tax the rich!" This slogan was prominent in Boston's Oct. 15, 2011 antiwar march, swelled to large size by many youth from Occupy Boston. The slogan cut through the mountains of confused verbiage on deficit reducation spewed forth by mainstream politicians, economists and journalists to give an incisive and accurate analysis. Furthermore, numerous polls showed that a majority of the American people support exactly this approach.

The identification of the primary source of problems in US society being the 1%—Wall Street, the banks and the financial institutions in particular—is a profoundly accurate insight of the Occupy movement. It dovetails with the Marxist analysis of the domination of finance capital widely accepted since the publication of Lenin's *Age of Imperialism* almost 100 years ago. Many Americans including labor are upset and angry about the domination of American public life by the Wall Street ruling elite. The Occupy movement articulated this feeling—with vivid, media-friendly imagery—and thus the large amount of support among the public. The Occupy sloganeers deserve congratulations!

Nationally, the occupy movement has been a big success in changing the political conversation to focus on economic injustice, Wall Street and corporate domination, and undemocratic control. While the occupy focus is not on peace issues, nonetheless United for Peace and Justice (UFPJ), comments that occupy has created "new openings and strategies" and is a "growing and powerful force for cultural change." The US Campaign to End the Israeli Occupation promotes Occupy AIPAC! to counter the AIPAC national convention in March 2012. The US Campaign has enthusiastically joined forces with the occupy movement by initiating teach-ins and supplying information packets. US Labor Against War features news about the occupy movement on its website, leading with a quote from the general secretary of the International Trade Union Confederation, "Occupy the US, not Iraq or Afghanistan."

*'Puppetista' at Fort Benning Protest*

In Boston, virtually every organization in the peace movement supports Occupy, whether mainstream-oriented budget cutters or leftwing communists taking to the streets. This is has been a good influence to bring people together, the 99%. Of course, there are many differences among the 99%, and dealing with some of these differences such as connecting with inner city folks and dealing with racism has been a challenge for Occupy Boston. Nonetheless, the 99% has been an effective slogan to emphasize that the people have many basic interests in common. There has been an amazing amount of press coverage from the encampment in Boston's downtown to its dispersal, even if not all accurate.

Peace activists in Boston organized a number of well-received events at the Dewey Square occupation site: a vigil marking ten years since the attack on Afghanistan; a standout supporting Palestinian rights; a teach-in on cutting the military budget. The peace movement has found Occupy Boston to be sympathetic and overall antiwar, supporting the ending of wars and efforts to cut the military budget and fund social needs.

## The '2nd Tier' Problem

However, peace and solidarity issues are definitely "second tier"—there is not much depth of understanding of the connections to domestic repression and injustice and pursuing this track is a second priority. The main Occupy issues are the power of corporations and economic inequality, democracy and the lack of it, and youth issues. Consequently a major thrust of United for Justice with Peace (Boston) working with Occupy Boston is education, showing the connections among the issues, and building Occupy Boston's Free School University. In January 2012 FSU sponsored a program on the situation in Iraq (combat troops withdrawn but 16,000 US personnel remain). Other programs are about drones and future Pentagon strategy, and peace and the economy.

The consensus decision-making process and horizontal democracy of Occupy are a variant of the organizing techniques of the global justice movement (1999 Seattle demonstration and after) and the Social Forums. Those movements have been effective in holding large, short-term events but have not been good on follow-through and building ongoing structure and mechanisms. This is now the challenge for the occupiers: how to sustain their movement.

In Boston, indoor meeting spaces for general assemblies have been located especially in churches, and the GA's continue to be well attended even after dispersal from the campsite. Occupy Boston has joined in with considerable energy the movement against fare hikes in public transportation, opposing housing evictions, and many other issues. The question remains, what will be the focus for Occupy's American Spring? Numerous internal meetings in Occupy Boston are discussing future plans and improving process to facilitate participation.

The occupation movement has youthful energy, appeals broadly, is colorful and participatory. Nonetheless it is missing an element of structure, appropriate leadership, and continuity. If the democratic socialists can embrace the body of Occupy, appreciating its great accomplishments and respecting its integrity, but also add some traditional socialist organizational skills and the analytic power of Marxism, then this combination could be a contribution to the development of the progressive majority and 21st century socialism.

*Duncan McFarland is the Treasurer of United for Justice with Peace in Boston, and a national committee member of CCDS*

# Vets Unplugged:
# Hoosier Anti-war Activist Connects
# Returning Veterans to the 99%

## By Harry Targ

"I grew up in Chicago and Northwest Indiana. Working-class family, father was a Union Ironworker... mother was a stay at home Mom." Vince Emanuele joined the Marines after graduating from high school. "I came out of boot camp a hard chargin' Devil Dog."

He served in the Marines from 2003 until 2005 stationed in California, Kuwait, and Iraq. His eight month deployment in Iraq involved him in street patrols, looking for snipers and land mines, "along with shooting at innocent civilians, destroying their property and beating up prisoners."

While in Iraq the fascination with war that he had acquired as a kid playing video games dissipated. His father sent him reading material—Noam Chomsky, Gore Vidal, Hunter Thompson, *The Nation*—and he and friends began to reflect on what they were doing in Iraq. He came to the view that the war was "illegal, immoral, unjustified, and unneeded." He was not spreading "democracy" or "peace" and the U.S. war effort was not winning the "hearts and minds" of the Iraqi people.

After returning to the U.S., Emanuele joined Iraq Veterans Against the War, has been organizing vets in Indiana and Illinois, created a weekly radio show called "Veterans Unplugged" which is available on-line, and has become a prominent activist for social, economic, and political justice in the heartland of America while finishing an undergraduate political science degree.

Emanuele recently spoke on a panel organized by the Lafayette Area Peace Coalition. He elaborated on the current plight of veterans, particularly veterans who served in the two longest wars in U.S. history, Afghanistan and Iraq.

While acknowledging that the current military force has chosen to enlist in regular army or reserve units, the 21st century enticement to serve is really an "economic draft." With declining incomes, wages, job opportunities, and rising educational costs, more and more men and women, he said, have seen military service as the only escape from lives of economic marginalization.

He spoke of the culture of militarization to which every new recruit is exposed: a process of dehumanization; the spread of racism, particularly targeting stereotypes of Muslims; sexism; and homophobia. In reality the military experience of young people, Emanuele said, involves placing raw, uneducated, teenagers in a war zone, with weapons and a license to kill. The victims of the actions of these raw recruits, schooled in video games and super-patriotism, were the millions of Iraqi and Afghan citizens who most fervently wanted the young foreigners off their land.

## Ongoing Impact of War on Vets

Emanuele presented some figures on the impacts of military service on returning veterans. (According to the Bureau of Labor Statistics in 2010 there were 20.2 million men and 1.8 million women who had served in the military). In 2011, Emanuele reported:

Rates of unemployment of returning veterans from Afghanistan and Iraq are higher than in the non-veteran population, both men and women; African-American vets experience double the unemployment rate of white vets; 80,000 returning veterans are currently homeless (56 % of homeless vets are African American or Latino); 20% to 50% of 21st century returning veterans suffer some form of Post Traumatic Stress Syndrome (an estimated 350,000 to 1 million vets); 1,000 returning vets attempt suicide each month.

Emanuele connected the plight of returning veterans to the military-industrial complex and imperial wars. As a member of Iraq Veterans Against the War, he highlighted the long tradition of soldiers resisting participation in unjust wars. He referred to patterns of resistance to war running throughout U.S. history:

In 1781 the Pennsylvania militia mutinied against war profiteers and for food; Between the 1870s and the 1890s, National Guard soldiers often refused to fire on striking workers; In 1919 unknown numbers of U.S. soldiers refused orders to go fight against the Bolsheviks who had come to power in Russia; Thousands of World War I veterans, known as the Bonus Army, assembled in Washington D.C. in 1932 to demand back pay due them from their active duty experience; From 1964-75 a massive GI anti-Vietnam war resistance movement emerged with over 300 GI anti-

*Vince Emanuele*

war newspapers produced, 10 % of all Vietnam era soldiers going AWOL or deserting, and a broad array of other forms of anti-war resistance and opposition to military recruiting.

Emanuele stressed the commonality of experience and vision that is shared by most veterans with the Occupy Movement. He suggested that peace and justice activists must understand that returning veterans are a vital part of the 99% movement committed to radically restructuring American society.

He argued that the 99%, including vets, must see the vital connections between the global capitalist system, the military-industrial complex, and the pain and suffering that have generated war and economic insecurity in the 21st century.

Emanuele ended his talk with reference to the frank admission of General Smedley Butler who oversaw the effort to crush the army of Augusto Sandino in Nicaragua in the early 1930s. Butler admitted that he, as a Marine General, had served as an instrumentality of Wall Street, putting down popular rebellions in the service of profit.

To learn more about Vince Emanuele and his weekly radio show check out Veterans Unplugged. To learn more about Iraq Veterans Against the War, go to the IVAW website.

***Harry Targ is a political science professor at Purdue University. He is a member of the national committee of CCDS, and blogs at Diary of a Heartland Radical -- and that's also the name of his new book which can be found at Lulu.com. Read more of Harry Targ's articles on The Rag Blog.***

# Love & Socialism: Observations from a Tour of Occupation Sites

## By Rael Pizarro

This past January, Alex—a young Boston Occupy activist and CCDS member—and I travelled down the East Coast and up through the South on a tour of as many Occupation sites as we could get to. We got to Manchester, New Hampshire, Philadelphia, Atlanta, New Orleans, Memphis and Lexington, Kentucky. We were honored to have been asked to speak at gatherings organized by CCDS leaders in Greensville, North Carolina and Lexington.

In Atlanta, I found a group of homeless people—including one family—living in what was left of the Occupation site in the Mid-Town section of the city. Memphis was very like Atlanta in that respect. In both cities, Occupiers were off attending other meetings, working and attending school; sometimes all of these things. But they didn't live in the encampment anymore. Those still living in the camp were otherwise without homes.

After introducing myself to the first person I saw, I was directed to Tony, a late 30-ish young man with whom I was told could speak best about the Occupation. He was squatting at the opening of his pup-tent, talking with Pierre, who sat on a chair just outside the opening. It was chilly - in the 30s. Rain was threatening and the ground was damp where we sat.

### Talking Socialism

My first thing was always to say that I was there for three reasons: to learn about the camp; to talk about socialism and the CCDS; and to see if they needed anything we could find a way to get them. The most immediate need was out of our hands—homes—but the city was also threatening to close the largest shelter, just a couple of blocks down the street from the encampment. Clearly, this group has special needs but I thought they were also making a special contribution to the movement, especially when I saw the dedication of people like Tony throughout the tour. I met many homeless people who were knowledgeable, committed and hopeful, despite their dire conditions.

Tony told me of the work they'd been doing stopping foreclosures. They'd had a string of victories in that area. The first was a house where the father who owned the mortgage had recently died. They also saved the home of a Sergeant in the state police. Most recently they'd saved a historic church that served the African-American community for 108-years. This made quite a bit of local press, including a long piece in the major paper and a television news report. Tony also told me about the increasing cooperation between the Black churches and Occupy. They'd attended a rally together—"Execute The Death Penalty"—where over fifty activists were arrested. These guys, including the homeless, were doing some serious work here.

We talked about socialism. Well, I talked about it and Tony nodded in agreement. I gave Tony a stack of CCDS newsletters before we had hugs all around and I left. As I walked away, I heard him hawking the paper, yelling out, "Take a newspaper! We're all socialists here!" Another took the Boston "We're The 99%" stickers and started handing them out.

Before I'd left on the trip, I'd heard many warnings not to use the 'S' word. Friends and comrades were concerned that the word carried connotations that would put off the less radical. Forget Communism. Forget class struggle. It's true also that when I asked the gathering in Greensboro who of them defined themselves as socialists, just a couple of hands went up. But those and a few others raised their hands when I asked who were members of the CCDS. Interesting. Maybe I wasn't clear about my question because I didn't see anything like this on the rest of the trip. The reaction was usually very different.

## No 'Fear' of Socialism

Putting aside for the moment how to deal with the baggage these words bring, I learned that there seemed to be no such concern with Socialism as such, the name or the concept, especially among the young people who are running this movement. Many already describe themselves as socialists, just as some indentify with Anarchism (though the latter are way outnumbered in the non-big-city Occupations) and the rest are open and curious to hear more about it. Like Alex said when I clumsily asked him about socialism for the first time back in Boston, "I'm not afraid of the word." It's only people my age and older that afraid of the word 'socialism'. The young are looking for solutions and socialism is one of several options. As different as each Occupation is one from another, this holds true for all.

*United mass mobilization in North Carolina*

Another common theme among all the Occupations, from Boston to Austin (I didn't see this in Manchester), is a difficulty each is having holding their group together without the focus of the physical Occupation. Predictably, those Occupations that continue to turn out people to public actions have much less of this problem. At first glance, they seem to be cities with histories of struggles. I'm thinking of Philadelphia, Atlanta, Lexington. In those places, there's much less in-fighting because they're focused on a common enemy. Most of the time.

There are divisions caused by insertion of identity politics, personality differences and fights over the question of non-violence. All of these have led to vitriol and paralysis of the already cumbersome decision-making process. Fortunately, there's the focus of what will inevitably be called The American Spring. This will keep the majority of current activists within the movement and a lot of amazing stuff can happen.

But there are concerns even beyond the spring. In New Orleans, I walked back from a meeting to where I was staying, with a young South Asian man. He expressed the same concern to me that Alex did earlier, that Occupy would complicate this year's elections and even take votes away from Obama. This is clearly one area where we distinguish ourselves and win allies and supporters. In the Southeast, we can be much more open about electoral politics than the Northern Occupations.

## Debates Over Non-Violence

And the question of violence vs. non-violence comes up again and again. It's expected that, whatever happens now, this issue will re-emerge with a vengeance in the spring and after. This leads me to the use of another word that's had a very positive and powerful impact on people: love. I believe that this is a revolution of love. I ask people, "Have you ever gotten so many hugs before?" Are you aware of what's happening in Maynmar right now? Was Gandhi and King not enough? We old-timers often associate that word, in a political context, with hippies sticking flowers in the business ends of gun barrels and people having sex in groups while covered in mud. "Make Love, Not War," sounds so jaded, so Woodstock, so yesterday, so naïve.

And yet, I found that this is mostly a problem with the men, young and old. Maybe it's not so much disagreement with the concept, but rather a difficulty expressing it in public discourse. The women loved it. They nodded their heads vehemently and smiled broadly, in both New Orleans and Lexington. My hope is that this love is used to counter violence and hate. That's what it's best at.

In summary: Some of the things I took away from the trip are: There are a great deal of homeless people in this movement and they have a lot to contribute and a lot of needs; some groups are having difficulty holding it together during this lull, but many great activists are sticking to it; the young have no problem with the words 'socialism,' 'revolution' or 'class struggle' and are open to discussions on them; they're grateful for any help you give them; there are anarchists in the Occupation groups in the South, but much less, proportionately and absolutely, than in the large Northern-city Occupations; there are many other differences; many cities in the South - and this is not very different in the North - have very few people of color, even though they abound in youth; that peace and love resonates with many, especially the young.

Most importantly, however, I learned that there's only so much you can learn hitting a couple of cities every day. I look forward to going back.

*Rael Pizarro is a trade union organizer in the Boston area, as well as a founding member of CCDS and one of its early co-chairs.*

# Occupy! Meets the Superbowl and the 'Right to Work for Less' in Indiana

*By Harry Targ*

*"The heart of the Super Bowl action will be in downtown Indianapolis at the three-block interactive fan environment known as Super Bowl Village. AFC and NFC fans, families, visitors and locals alike can enjoy this ultimate, free fan zone that spans from Bankers Life Fieldhouse all the way to the NFL Experience at the Indiana Convention Center via the newly redesigned Georgia Street.*

*"In addition to endless entertainment, interactive games, Tailgate Town, live concerts on two different stages, bars and other attractions, fans can also fly over Super Bowl Village with four zip lines that traverse Capitol Avenue." -- VisitIndy.com*

WEST LAFAYETTE, Indiana—One hundred passionate activists from labor and occupy groups around the state of Indiana assembled at the State House on Saturday, January 28, to continue opposition to the pending "Right-to-Work-for-Less" bill which appears to be close to final endorsement by the legislature and Indiana Governor Mitch Daniels.

Ironically, Alcoa Corporation just announced the expansion of plant facilities in Lafayette, Indiana, prior to the passage of the odious anti-worker bill that Governor Daniels has claimed will bring more jobs to Indiana. A plant in Iowa, a Right-to-Work State, lost its bid for the Alcoa plant expansion to Indiana, not yet such a state. Workers in the Lafayette plant are represented by United Steel Workers of America Local 115.

## Battle at the State house

The Indiana House of Representatives last week voted 54-44 to endorse a Right-To-Work bill (several Republicans voted "no" with their Democratic colleagues). Now the bill returns to the Indiana Senate for discussion of amendments to the bill and final passage before it goes to the desk of the Governor for his signature. Despite the fact that he had promised labor in the past that he would not support such a bill, the Governor made it his top priority item in the 2012 legislative session.

The intense political battle over RTW has occurred in the context of enormous celebration of the impending arrival of 150,000 NFL fans to the

Super Bowl which will be played in Indianapolis on Sunday, February 5. Indianapolis big money interests have been lobbying for this event for years, hoping to put the city on the map for hosting huge money-making events such as the football classic.

Two buses of anti-RTW protesters traveled from Lafayette, Indiana, and Purdue University, 65 miles away, to the rally. After spirited speeches, including remarks from three state legislators, representatives from building trades unions, students, and professors, rally organizers led a march through the Super Bowl village in downtown Indianapolis. Marchers were seen by thousands of Super Bowl celebrants who were roaming around the village spending money in dozens of food and entertainment venues.

Demonstrators encountered some hostile reactions, including physical jostling, but also numerous thumbs up and clenched fists in support of protestors carrying placards demanding "Kill the Bill," "Workers United Will Prevail," and "Occupy Purdue."

## A Long History

Opposition to Right-to-Work has a decade-long history around the state since the governorship and the Indiana House of Representatives has shifted from Republican to Democrat and then Republican control. The Republicans, for their part, are committed to destroying the labor movement not only to reduce labor costs but also to end political opposition to their domination of state government.

Among the responses has been the Indiana Coalition for Worker Rights initiated by the Northwest Central Labor Council, AFL-CIO, in 2006, "to educate and mobilize workers to demand and defend worker rights." It pledged itself to:

educate union members and the public about the negative consequences of "Right-to-Work (for Less)" legislation; challenge the general shift toward privatization of public institutions such as schools, libraries, and health care delivery systems; mobilize citizens to support a living wage for all workers, affordable health care and education, and greater worker rights to participate in the workplace and the political system; and work with others to create a coalition of informed citizens "who believe that the protection of workers' rights is the bedrock of our democratic society."

In the summer of 2011, a coalition representing various progressive groups in the Greater Lafayette community formed to work on reproductive health care, civil liberties, peace, and labor rights. The new organization, the Indiana Rebuild the American Dream Coalition, held jobs and justice rallies in downtown Lafayette in November.

Parallel to these developments the Tippecanoe Building and Construction Trades AFL-CIO and Occupy Purdue and Occupy Lafayette have mobilized around Right-to-Work and a whole range of issues that concern the 99 per cent.

It is clear from the experiences of small communities such as those in Tippecanoe County (Lafayette and West Lafayette are the population centers) and various other communities all across Indiana that so-called "outside" and "inside" strategies are needed to fight back against the draconian efforts to destroy worker rights, to promote acceptable living conditions for all, and to begin to create a better world.

Outside strategies include mass mobilizations, protests, educational forums, and dramatic public displays of peoples' views in venues such as the Super Bowl celebrations.

Jim Ogden, Lafayette, union electrician from IBEW Local 668, articulated a strategy of how best to connect the mass mobilizations to electoral work, a so-called "inside strategy":

We realize that at this point where it's at in the legislation. We probably will not stop this.

At this point, I think we're looking at this as a kickoff for the elections in November. And trying to do whatever we can to get the Republicans that had voted for this, to get them out of office. (Journal and Courier, January 29, 2012)

It is clear that the electoral process cannot alone defend workers' rights. However, in the context of the immediate needs of the 99 percent, elections, in conjunction with massive public expressions of protest, must constitute a critical component of the work of progressives in the months ahead.

*Harry Targ is a professor of political science at Purdue University who lives in West Lafayette, Indiana. He blogs at Diary of a Heartland Radical -- and that's also the name of his new book which can be found at Lulu.com. Read more of Harry Targ's articles on The Rag Blog.*

# Occupy Wall Street: Openings to Worker-Occupation of Factories and Enterprises in the U.S.

*By Peter Ranis*

## The Social Economy Context

The Occupy Wall Street (OWS) movement has clearly expressed the hopes and great potentialities of the working class both in the U.S. and globally. The 99 percent are speaking up and saying that they will no longer do the bidding of the 1 percent. In essence it is the revolt of the masses, the underclass in their many guises. People in NYC's Zuccotti Park are doing incredible things autonomously and with purpose. They  are developing an island of political and economic autonomy that draws attention to what people can do on their own and for themselves. From many walks of life they are standing up and speaking with measured purpose and being heard. This is a valuable lesson for the American working class and their right to stand up and defend their jobs in factories and enterprises from being "disappeared."

The crash and recession of 2008 only heightened the concerns that we have about the capacity and willingness of liberal capital to provide for justice and equity for the overwhelming majority of Americans. The lack of societal concern by the large hierarchical capitalist firms and financial institutions has never been so clearly manifested. OWS represents a momentous breakthrough that demonstrates that we can indeed come together at this crucial time as workers, social movements, intellectuals, and labor unions, and use this critical opening to move forward to confront capital-labor relations throughout America.

The U.N. has declared 2012 the International Year of Cooperatives. This only adds to the imperative for exploring the many ways that worker-managed factories and enterprises can be seen as an alternative to traditional capitalist firms and companies. Cooperatives as worker-managed enterprises, for a number of institutional and societal reasons, represent alternative productive vehicles attempting to override the impact of deindustrialization, globalization, and the neoliberal ideological offensive. The social economy and solidarity relationships, represented by worker-managed enterprises, need to be examined as focal points for working-class and middle-class capacities to sustain the possibilities of a productive worker-centered culture. This has become ever more urgent given the shrinkage of labor union density, especially the decline of private-sector organized workers. Worker-managed factories and enterprises are called for particularly at this moment with the declining industrial base of the American working class. Perhaps upward of 25% of the American industrial heartland lies idle with the potential for unemployed workers to create cooperatives and other self-managed enterprises to fill that vacuum. But they need not be limited to laborers. The large bulk of the American working class find themselves in the services, in commerce, and among contingent workers, subcontracted workers, and immigrant workers. All of these groups deserve the benefits and entitlements that capital-labor reorganization would provide them.

Workers need to embrace the knowledge that worker-managed workplaces are a realistic and grounded alternative. Certainly in countries such as Argentina, Spain, Venezuela, Brazil, and Canada, worker self-managed companies have asserted themselves as new forms of worker solidarity, autonomy, and participatory initiatives within the capitalist economy. The experiences of the 21st century's first decade demonstrate that class consciousness and political awakening are enhanced, not diminished, by workers banding together into economic units that depend upon working-class and middle-class economic initiatives providing new forms of penetrating and mediating the challenges of the capitalist marketplace.

## The Worker-Management Alternative

There are many reasons to be positive about the feasibility, continuity, and longevity of the major innovations among cooperatives and recuperated enterprises. These constitute participatory worker involvement in managing enterprises, worker direct democracy through periodic assemblies, job rotations and reskilling, and educational and cultural outreach to community groups, social movements, and labor unions.[1]

Research, particularly in Argentina, points to a heightened involvement among the cooperative and recuperated enterprise workers in public policy and its implications for the working class writ large.[2] I have observed that workers in Argentine cooperatives have a far better sense than other workers, even those unionized, in relating their working lives with other roles they play as community citizens and political activists, thus broadening their societal place.

There is clear evidence from the Spanish and Argentine cases that workers can organize and run the means of production while retaining equity and justice for the employees involved. Income distribution is not skewed to the top, management salaries and short-term profit taking by owners as well as managers are avoided, and capital is thus constantly reinvested in the firm itself. Cooperatives also serve as schools for participatory democracy as workers self-manage their work life, the largest investment of time in their daily lives.[3]

The world's leading industrial cooperative, the Spanish Mondragon multinational cooperative, serves as an emblematic case of what can be achieved. Judith D. Schwartz writes:

> One hallmark of the Mondragon model is its use of capital. Rather than flowing into the pockets of executives and outside investors, a company's profits are distributed in a precise, democratic way; set aside as seed money for new cooperatives; distributed to regional nonprofits; or pooled into shared institutions like the university and research center. In other words each individual cooperative gains long-term benefits from the financial assets of the whole.[4]

Cooperatives are also better organized and sustained by values foreign to typical venture capital firms and thus are much more likely to withstand economic crisis such as the U.S. economy experienced in 2008. Robb, Smith, and Webb argue persuasively:

> As the world learned in September 2008, as the value of investor owned publicly traded shares dropped by 20-40%, the unlimited return may be negative as a result of the unregulated pursuit of narrow self interest. Cooperative financial institutions did not create any of the "toxic paper" nor did the value of cooperative shares decline. The absence of cooperatives from this massive malfeasance and turmoil are additional benefits of deploying capital as cooperative capital. Those benefits accrue to both individuals using cooperatives to meet their needs and to the public generally. They are public policy benefits.

They go on to say:

> The founders of the Mondragon cooperative wanted to create workplaces that were participatory and to stop the drain of people from the region. Since launching its first cooperative in 1956 the Mondragon group has grown to a workforce of 92,700 in 2008. The Caja [bank] has successfully participated in the growth of the Mondragon cooperative while achieving a solid success as a finan-

cial institution. In 1988 it administered 1.3 billion Euros and by 2008 that had grown to 13.9 billion Euros.[5]

The proliferation of OWS from New York City to Oakland and beyond testifies to the yearning for more democratic and participatory means of existence. Moreover, public opinion has cast a favorable eye on these movements as they are touching deep-seated needs among all sectors of society.[6] The OWS represents a progressive challenge to finance and corporate capital by focusing on their multiple defects rather embracing a reflexive anti-capitalist jargon. By the same token, where cooperatives have flourished, they represent a radical challenge to public policy by not beginning with a generalized, diffuse left-critique of capitalism without a clear and defined entry point. Recuperated enterprises by workers combine a left outlook that has a majoritarian basis because its demands and needs are so reasonable yet comprehensive. They typify the real frustrations of the unemployed and the potentially unemployed and should receive the sympathy and support of most citizenry in any capitalist country. The Wisconsin mobilizations, the Arab Spring, and the Spanish general strikes, as well as the proliferation of OWS, constitute a left-populist insurgency that bodes well for a push against corporate capital and its minions.

## The Deindustrialization Crisis in the U.S.

The U.S. crisis of unemployment and underemployment, 16% by 2011,[7] is probably more severe than at any time, including the Great Depression, because of the special and novel structural nature of unemployment caused by a global-oriented capitalist sector, the spread of technology throughout the world, and the increasing competition from skilled, low-wage workers abroad. Since the onset of the recession of 2008, 15% of the U.S. industrial sector jobs have been lost. Growing free trade deficits arising from the NAFTA alone have caused the loss of almost 700,000 U.S. jobs, most of them in manufacturing.[8]

What is required is a fundamental reorientation of the responsibility of public policy-making in defending the American working class. This has been essentially an absent ingredient. James Galbraith has written of the American predator state in which the wealthy class has taken over the government and legitimized certain approaches to the U.S. economy, among them monetarism, supply-side tax cuts, balanced budgets, and free trade. The underlying philosophy of the predator state is the inviolability of private property as exempt from heavy taxation.[9] Robert Skidelsky has contended that Keynesian economic thought revolving around fiscal economic interventions has been categorically pushed aside since the Reagan presidency to the detriment of the U.S. industrial policy. He argues that the Bretton-Woods Keynesian era of 1951-1973

**Fagor Cooperative Factory in Mondragon**

was superior to the Washington Consensus periods in terms of GDP growth rates, absence of recessions, lower unemployment, and more income equality. In contradiction to neoclassical economists in the U.S., he demonstrates that, despite the better growth rates, lower unemployment and greater income equality of the former, there was no difference in inflation rates between these two periods.[10]

The contemporary role of government has been ambivalent in restoring public and private employment as has its reaction to outsourcing and offshoring. A Democratic administration, confronting a demonically cynical, neo-conservative House of Representatives, has not embraced fundamental initiatives that would reconstruct a declining industrial economy. My view is that we need a serious change in the direction of the state. As has been shown by OWS and its Wisconsin predecessor, it has become increasingly evident that concerted activism can highlight the challenge by heralding the potential power of the solidarity economy. We need to examine the areas in which progressive community, political, and legal activists, with the cooperation of public agencies and city councils, can come together as advocates for working-class and middle-class empowerment.

In the U.S. context, the deep economic recession beginning in 2008 with double-digit unemployment both nationally and in various hitherto industrial states offers a rare combination of structural and ideological openings for reintroducing New Deal-style executive and legislative interventions. It is significant that the rise of worker cooperatives in Argentina followed on the heels of the financial default and economic crisis of 2001 fueled by rampant deindustrialization, high unemployment, and a dramatic growth of poverty and indigence.

## The Argentine Example

In Argentina, workers have asserted their right to take over factories on the basis of national and provincial constitutional law that allows for the takeover of private enterprises with reasonable compensation in the interest of the "common good" and "public use." These actions occur when there is clear evidence that the effects of economic recession are fraudulently used by owners to decapitalize and disinvest in their firms. Some owners have reaped millions of dollars in government credits for non-production-related financial speculation while breaking labor contracts with workers and depriving them of their earned wages. Still others simply walked away from their enterprises by declaring bankruptcy and then, unburdened by financial duress, began new ones with unorganized cheaper labor. Expropriation by Argentine provincial or municipal legislatures on a case-by-case basis gives the cooperative workers protection from the creditors' demands upon the previous owners who incurred any possible debts. Without expropriation creditors can demand the auctioning off of the buildings and their contents, throwing the workers into the streets. 60% of the worker cooperatives have been given legal protection by provincial expropriations.[11] In some cases bankruptcy court rulings allow the workers to commence production as compensation for lost wages and benefits or allow for rental or lease agreements—always under the legal usage of the right to set up worker cooperatives. In a few exceptional cases, workers themselves purchase the bankrupt enterprise over time.[12]

It should not be lost on the OWS movement that the watchword for Argentine workers recuperating their factories was "Occupy, Resist, and Produce!" In many cases workers occupied the factories that were about to be abandoned by their owners and sought support from neighbors, community networks, social movements, public-spirited lawyers, and progressive left political parties with a history of militancy. Once established, workers banding together can almost always make a go of the recuperated factory or enterprise by a significant shift in working-class cultural values and orientations. Workers working collectively, rather than competing individually to please managers and bosses, a climate of fostering a team mentality becomes possible. In a recuperated worker cooperative, knowledge of the enterprise's resources necessary for production, deeper knowledge of the product itself, and an understanding of the challenges to market the product become more widely dispersed among the workforce. The workers are involved in the hiring of new co-operative members, participate in the discipline of those working, and have the increasing potential to participate in questions of reinvestment or redistribution of the profits. Information is no longer held by capital-ist owners and managers as a wedge of power applied against the work-ers but generously shared with those workers with a vocation and appe-tite for enhanced understanding of the production process.

The rate of continuity of Argentine cooperatives as of 2008 was 93% with only a 7% mortality rate.[13] They have managed to carve out areas of economic survival that attests to worker initiative, collective engage-ment, and reconfiguring the workplace. As the workers proceed in the occupation and recuperation of their workplaces, they are touching on fundamental questions concerning the direction of the neoliberal econ-omy. As the legal advisor to the 480-member Zanón/Fasinpat ceramic workers cooperative told me, "If there were 100 Zanóns this would be a different country. Zanón is struggling not to be just another factory but to be the leading edge of social change in Argentina."[14] By their capacity to form alliances with progressive legal, community, political, and labor forces available to them, they symbolize an alternative path to economic development that is predicated on worker solidarity and democracy in the workplace. The collective ownership of the workplace acts as a cultural catalyst for worker sacrifice, ingenuity, and creativity. Workers often originally formed cooperatives to avoid unemployment and poverty.[15] Nevertheless through struggle and sacrifice they become socialized to a novel working class culture they are willing to defend. I argue that this model can be duplicated in the United States.

The University of Buenos Aires amassed a comprehensive study on the current state of Argentine recuperated enterprises.[16] The number of en-terprises recuperated as cooperatives increased from 161 in 2004 to 205 in 2010, and the numbers of workers so employed and officially documented increased from 7,000 to 9,400.[17] Once the recuperated enterprises become cooperatives, legitimized by provincial and munici-pal expropriation laws, they demonstrate impressive solidarity among themselves by way of inter-cooperative associations, community and neighborhood groups, and a scattering of political parties and social movements such as the piqueteros (representing the poor and unem-ployed who take direct action to express their grievances).[18] Though the Argentine national state has not been the initiator of the recuperated enterprise movement, it has not obstructed its development. Though the support has not been overwhelming, ministries in the federal gov-ernment as well as those of various provinces and municipalities have intervened with subsidies, worker training, and legal counseling as well as social welfare programs. There has also been support from the public at large by way of donations, client help, food contributions, and political party pro bono advice.[19]

The overwhelming majority of the newly formed worker cooperatives meet either weekly or monthly to appraise administrative and production policies. In addition the cooperatives revise and reorganize working conditions by job rotations and other strategies to humanize daily work habits. More than half of the cooperatives allow only 33% difference between the highest and lowest paid member and over half keep the difference to just 25% or less. The differentiations are understandably based on the functions performed by the worker, the hours worked, the specialized category stipulated by prior union contracts, and worker seniority.[20]

Many cooperatives open up their facilities to the community, creating specialized kindergartens, elementary and secondary schools, as well as student internship and training programs and even documentation centers and worker-oriented libraries.[21] Significantly, Argentine recuperated enterprises and cooperatives are important participants in social movements and are particularly active in cultural and educational outreach to their surrounding communities and neighborhoods. For example the Zanón/Fasinpat cooperative ceramic factory of Neuquén Province has created a community health clinic which it subsidizes; in the city of Buenos Aires, Maderera Córdoba has created a cooperative woodworking secondary school and IMPA (Industria Metalúrgica y Plástica de Argentina) an adult education curriculum; the Chilavert printing cooperative opens its space to publishing workshops, literary readings, and art exhibits; and the Hotel Bauen cooperative facilitates space for community groups to present artistic, cultural, and political events.[22]

## Eminent Domain and the Solidarity Economy

In the U.S. we have the same mechanism as exists in Argentina to achieve worker-owned and worker-managed factories and enterprises: eminent domain. Eminent domain is constitutionally sanctioned and has been applied for community, infrastructure, and development purposes. Plant closings have severe negative economic repercussions and societal externalities on workers and communities. These events then legitimize the right to regulate them by way of eminent domain on behalf of the public interest.

The collective social rights of workers who have built up the value of the firm through years of hard work and applying their know-how and skills have to be legally asserted. The companies cannot be free of societal obligations. By outsourcing jobs they have broken a contract for which there must be reparations and consequences. The use of eminent

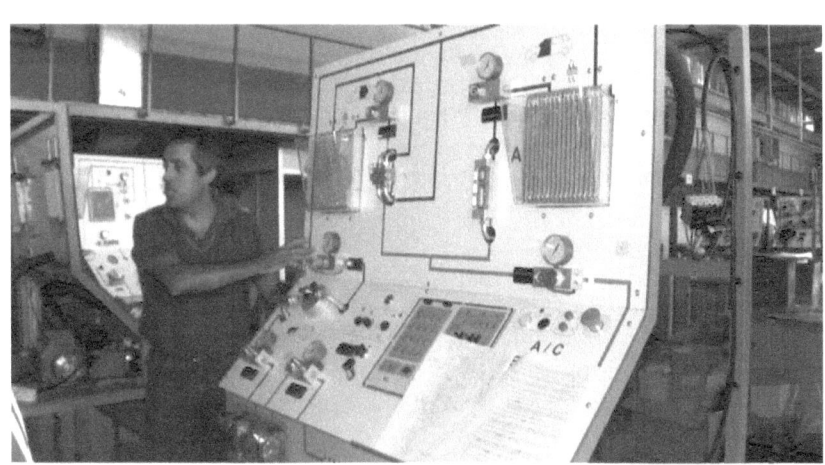

**Student-worker explains teaching machine that his team created in Mondragon**

domain can spark a public debate about the obligations of corporations and confront the passive acceptance of the steady decline of jobs with livable wages.

Although there are thousands of credit, consumer, housing, utility, insurance, and agricultural cooperatives in the U.S. servicing millions of Americans,[23] there are only about 300 small worker cooperatives in which workers are truly involved in the day-to-day organization and participation in production and services. The use of eminent domain can provide the impetus to put worker-owned and worker-managed enterprises into the critical discussion of recovering jobs in America. In a landmark decision for the struggling American working class, the U.S. Supreme Court in Kelo v. New London (2005) ruled in favor of the city of New London by reason of eminent domain to take over private property for reasons of "public purpose." The court ruled on behalf of New London's economic development plan based on the "takings clause" of the U.S. Constitution's Fifth Amendment which states, ". . . nor shall private property be taken for public use, without just compensation." Justice John Paul Stevens wrote for the majority that expropriation of private holdings as part of urban development is justified for the public purpose of increasing jobs, tax revenues, and reversing urban decay. In a previous relevant case, Berman v. Parker (1954), a unanimous court observed: "The concept of public welfare is broad and inclusive." It becomes clear in Berman that the meaning of public use had been expanded to include "public interest" and "public welfare" by way of eliminating blight in a poverty-stricken neighborhood in Washington, D.C.

In the U.S. eminent domain has been used for many decades for building highways, airports, hospitals, municipal offices, schools, libraries, public parks, and sport complexes in the name of urban development and the public benefit. It is more appropriate to apply this same rationale to protect against the loss of industrial and service jobs on behalf of labor and the American working class.[24] What greater public purpose could there be than preserving work for the public! We need to use eminent domain for development purposes much as we use taxation and regulatory and zoning legislation.

Once expropriated, the factories and enterprises would then be turned over to the workers themselves who have the technical skills and know-how to run these industries. In Argentina, for example, workers have shown they can maintain and manage enterprises and industries, be they metal plants, tire factories, food processors, chemical plants, meat-packing plants, textile factories, auto parts installations, electronic component suppliers, ceramic factories, lumber factories, glass factories, supermarkets, printers and publishers, health clinics, hospitals, schools, and hotels as successful and viable establishments.

What distinguishes worker-run firms from traditional capitalist firms is that, in the former, workers achieve a greater knowledge of work procedures and the rationale for the entire production process. In addition workers enhance their knowledge of the enterprise budget through open assemblies that make the decisions concerning capital reinvestment versus profit distribution.

The formation of worker cooperatives via eminent domain provides a platform where worker productivity and wages move together, where shareholder dependency doesn't exist, where equity firms have no role. Cooperatives, for example, do not rely on equity capital which requires high rates of profit often resulting from nonproductive sources of revenue. Within the newly-formed cooperative structure, the previously very visible disjunction between full-time, part-time, and temporary workers is abolished. There is a basic modicum of worker security and worker alienation is substantially reduced. Without owners and privileged managers and their super-sized salaries, workers share the enhanced profits equitably. Where speedups and pay cuts are required everyone shares in the downturn; hours may be cut, salaries reduced, until profits are reestablished, but the decisions are made by a majority in worker assemblies and the workforce remains in place.

David Gutknecht has highlighted a salient difference between cooperatives and traditional capitalist firms: "Cooperatives keep capital in the community where it was generated, while stock companies export capital elsewhere. Since they give surplus revenue back to their members, cooperatives keep wealth in their communities. Stock companies do the reverse. By distributing profits to shareholders, they take capital out of the community."[25]

## Workers' Self-Empowerment in the U.S.

Legally, eminent domain can legitimize the worker-owned and worker-managed factories as they strive to maintain their jobs and salvage the enterprises for themselves and their communities, while organizing for the larger goal of defending industrial and enterprise development and viable employment within the U.S. We have seen examples of worker comprehension of their rights as the creators of capital and their rights to keep their industry and jobs when equity firms have sought to vacate the premises and break contracts with both workers and communities. We have the partial examples of the Republic Windows and Doors workers in Chicago in 2008-2009, the Stella D'Oro bakery workers in the Bronx, New York in 2008-2009, and the Taunton, MA Haskon Aerospace workers in 2010-2011 taking the crucial initial steps of sit-down strikes and factory occupations to oppose equity firms leaving the workers and communities behind (in these cases, equity firms Gillman, Brynwood, and Esterline took out equipment to cheaper sites in other states or other countries). The latter two plants, however, closed in the end, throwing 136 and 100 workers respectively into unemployment, and in the Chicago case, a new firm has taken ownership (Serious Materials) which has rehired only 10% of the former 260 workers.

Factory occupations, sit-ins, petitioning public authorities to save jobs, nevertheless, are the necessary backdrops to advocacy for the application of eminent domain procedures. The formation of worker cooperatives by the U.S. working and middle classes has a major potential if supported by labor unions and organizations of central and municipal labor councils combined with community and legal organizers and activists. Desperate times call for desperate measures, and factory and enterprise occupations need to be put on the immediate horizon. Workers must initiate eminent domain proceedings in every single case of a runaway ownership, making it de rigueur activity everywhere in the U.S., so that it becomes a reflexive, multiplier activity accepted as a legitimate response to arbitrary and irresponsible behavior by private owners.

The American public has shown in surveys that it supports tax increases to bridge budget deficits rather than decreasing pay and benefits to the working class or reducing health care, educational expenditure, or public transportation.[26] There is little question that public opinion would support workers defending their jobs and homes against equity firms whose commitment is not to any particular community or country but to itself and its investors. Chains of worker cooperatives could become regional interlacing industrial zones committed to each other's existence and survival with an outreach to ever wider communities in terms of educational, cultural, and job opportunities.

Civil society's need must take precedent over private property sanctity. The writings of William Blackstone in 18th century England gave credence to state obligations over John Locke's (17th century) view of the preeminence of the absolute of private property. Judicial decisions, stimulated by opinions by Justice Louis Brandeis, have broadened the redefinition of eminent domain from public use to public purpose, public needs, and public benefit. As Brandeis wrote "the rights of properties and individuals have to be remolded from time to time at the behest of the needs of society." Such interpretations of eminent domain were common in the progressive era, the New Deal Years, and even the Eisenhower years. We have the Supreme Court decisions in Berman (1954), Midkiff (1984), and Kelo (2005), plus the various state cases such as the Poletown v. City of Detroit case in Michigan (1981) and various private transportation and utility eminent domain proceedings in Minneapolis (1974), New York City (1976), Wisconsin (1978), and Connecticut (1982)—all strengthening the usage of the takings clause of the constitution for a greater public purpose be it for ending community blight, inequitable usage of land, economic development, and providing for a public need. It is only since the advent of Reaganomics that we have had John Locke's ideas imposed again via the Institute of Justice (1991), a right-wing think tank, and the Castle Coalition (2002), a right-wing advocacy group who have fastened on "eminent domain abuse" as a term of opprobrium which muddies the water of its positive usages and outcomes.

It is more and more obvious we cannot rely solely on the labor movement for grand initiatives, given that only 12% of our workforce is now unionized (8% of private-sector workers). It has to be the laborers, employees and middle-class workers representing 85% of Americans upon whom we base these aspirations.

As Occupy Wall Street has made clear, at present the American working class is subject to the overwhelming ideology of property rights, banking and business subsidies, flawed and give-back collective bargaining agreements, and at-will firings that inhibit their capacity for effectiveness as well as destroy their sustenance. Further we are under the aegis of neoclassical economists (Bernanke, Summers, et al.) who focus on the health of an economy as predicated on GNP growth whether it provides for jobs or not.

In December 2008, the United Electrical (UE) workers occupied the Chicago Republic Windows and Doors factory in protest against the company throwing its workers into the street without the two-month notice required by the 1988 WARN labor law. In Great Britain workers occupied three Visteon plants which supply parts for Ford Motor Company. In Ireland the Waterford Crystal plant was worker-occupied after it was bought out by a U.S. equity firm KPS. And in France, workers took bosses and managers hostages (so-called "bossnappings") for a day or over night in the French Caterpillar plant, a SM plant, a SONY plant, and a Michelin plant. All these protests resulted in either reducing the numbers of workers scheduled to be laid off, saved all jobs for a certain period, gained dramatically enhanced severance pay or promises of a new entity that would transfer and restore their jobs.[27]

The commonality in all these worker actions was the occupation of the factory or offices before attempting to negotiate with the owners and mangers. That gave the workers the legal, political, and ethical bargaining power to confront capital on its own playing field, namely by contending that the company is breaking a contract and a commitment to a community. And because of the dramatic nature of the workers' militancy, in all these cases of worker occupations of plants and managers' offices, the U.S., British, and French public officialdom got involved in the support of the workers: in Illinois state legislators, Chicago ward councilors, Senator Richard Durbin, Vice-President Joe Biden, and President Barack Obama supported the sit-down action; in Ireland, various Northern Ireland governmental ministers gave their support to the Visteon workers; and French President Nicolas Sarkozy made commitments that there would be no immediate layoffs. This influenced and solidified legal opinion, public support, and gave the workers the additional moral authority to push their demands.

## Beyond Factory Occupations

These are key first steps, but it is critical to take the second step and form a worker-managed enterprise and call for city or state legal action using eminent domain. Leaving the factory before securing political support and legal initiatives, as in the case of the courageous and defiant Stella D'Oro bakery workers on strike in the Bronx, New York in 2008-09, is not the best alternative. The 136 workers had shown themselves to be a coherent and solid group of workers, striking for 11 months to resist draconian job givebacks. Not a single worker crossed the picket line, while they engaged an important community, political, and labor support group and used its union, Local 50 of the Bakery Confectionery, Tobacco Workers, and Grain Millers (BCTGM) to attain a positive National Labor Relations Board (NLRB) ruling that mandated back pay and benefits. Almost immediately after the NLRB ruling in July 2009, Brynwood Partners, the equity firm that now owned Stella D'Oro, announced plans to close the factory and eventually sold it to the manufacturer, Lance, Inc. which moved the company to Ohio in the fall of 2009.

As important as the Stella D'Oro solidarity outreach was, it was not enough to save the jobs of the 136 workers. Without a decisive plant occupation, community groups and labor unions alone are not enough to carry the day. Concerted worker activism is the required first step followed by the use of eminent domain proceedings instituted by the municipalities involved. In New York City, however, neither the city council nor the mayor provided the necessary critical support. Had OWS been in place at that time, there is no doubt that this movement could have provided the necessary mobilization on behalf of these Bronx workers.

The UE Chicago workers took that first principled and reasonable step of peacefully occupying and maintaining the Republic plant ready for production. This stood as a powerful message and opportunity for the American working class to make that cultural leap. In February 2009 a bankruptcy court judge ruled that a California building materials company (Serious Materials) could purchase the plant's assets and employ the 260 workers involved in the occupation of the factory. However, this alternative was fraught with the uncertainty of market calculations by the private buyer. By mid 2010, Serious Materials had rehired only 30 workers. It would have again been appropriate if a progressive community and political coalition in Chicago had called for the intervention from the city council to implement eminent domain proceedings.[28]

In Taunton, MA, workers, again of the United Electrical Workers (UE), were in a serious labor conflict with Esterline Technologies, which planned to move 100 jobs to non-union plants in California and Mexico. The Taunton plant, Haskon, Inc, made door seals and silicon gaskets for aircraft. Despite being a profitable enterprise with profits of $120 million in 2010, Esterline announced it would auction off the equipment in December 2010 to pay for the workers' severance package. The UE was able to get the support of Congressman Barney Frank, state legislators, and the City Council to request a delay the auctioning of the Haskon equipment until mid-February 2011. For the first time in recent modern labor history, the union then attempted to initiate eminent domain proceedings, with the support of the Taunton City Council and the Mayor, to seize the Esterline machinery and buy the property and factory on behalf of the workers. According to the Massachusetts Constitution law of home rule, eminent domain can be applied to taking of property, both personal (machinery and equitment) and intangible.

This purposeful and creative methodology sadly failed for several reasons. Firstly, the Taunton City Council in late December 2010 passed a home rule petition sent to the Massachusetts legislature to apply the use of eminent domain to purchase the company machinery and equipment. A home rule petition became a necessary procedure because Esterline did not own the building, only the machinery and equipment. Secondly, the Esterline Company demanded $300,000 to pay the cost of the equipment and machinery from the Haskon workers to avoid an auction that would probably be worth a third of that. Thirdly, the auction occurred on January 19th, two days before the Massachusetts legislature reconvened to even consider an eminent domain intervention and the severance package was approved by the aerospace workers at Haskon.

Still, this labor confrontation in Taunton, MA showed the possibility of applying eminent domain to runaway plants. The UE and the workers were able to get the support of local unions, Jobs with Justice chapters, Massachusetts Nurses Association, Jewish Labor Committee, Greater Southeastern Massachusetts Labor Council, and community residents of Taunton. They were able to use this groundswell to get the City Council and Mayor to vote in favor of eminent domain and to get voices of support from state legislators as well as their congressional representative, Barney Frank. As in the Stella D'Oro case in Bronx, New York, an important factor was the certainty of a severance package as opposed to the challenges of the struggle, both political and financial, to see eminent domain proceedings to their conclusion. This requires a good deal of courage on the part of the workers involved as well as the willingness to depart from the norms of previous plant closing scenarios. Unless eminent domain becomes a manageable choice—a default alternative —severance payouts will continue to poorly compensate workers while closing their industries and commerce throughout America.

## The Occupy Wall Street Context

Cooperatives and recuperated enterprises are in the last analysis defensive strategies, but they allow the workers to act "as a class in itself and for itself" as Marx advocated. These structures combine human values of self-interest and survival with real democratic participatory life. Theoretical liberal democratic representative government has proven over time to be inadequate to the needs of workers. As the Occupy Wall Street movement shows, people are yearning for actual on-the-ground democratic participatory life, not just wishing to defend economic interests. In taking over factories and enterprises, workers can concretize the OWS movement, becoming protagonists who represent themselves and, in so doing, represent the overwhelming majority of people in any given community. When workers occupy a factory or enterprise, it is really about what they attempt to keep, not what they attempt to take. By dint of their work they have produced a product, raised capital and invested it, and supplied the surrounding community with their consumption, their taxes, and their everyday involvement in the life of their town or city. It is crucial to expand the narrow definition of private property. Whose property is it anyway? The erstwhile owners and managers who accumulated the original capital and initiated the investment proposal, or the workers who have made them usable and useful and magnified their value through years and often decades of commitment and hard work?

Workers cannot be separated from the capital they have produced. A necessary collective contract has developed over time that puts the workers in the forefront of who is responsible in the final analysis. This relationship or, really, social contract has superseded the simplistic notion of private property as belonging to the owner.

The implementation of eminent domain on behalf of the working class provides a sense of the workers as not only the legitimate owners of the enterprise but views workers as independently demanding equity and basic social justice. Deindustrialization in Argentina since the military regimes of 1976-83, followed by liberal and neo-liberal civil administrations in the 1980s and 1990s, led to the economic crisis of 2001. After the financial default and the explosion of unemployment and poverty in 2001-2002, cooperatives became a clear and necessary working-class choice in Argentina and the government helped workers recuperate enterprises, as discussed above. These conditions approximate those in the U.S. since the deep recession that began in 2008 and continues today to impact the U.S. working class that is undergoing a dramatic deterioration.[29]

We need to expand what is politically the right of the working class to occupy factories and offices when they are threatened with unwarranted closure based solely on the desire for more rapid accumulation of profit. There are examples, particularly in Argentina, that demonstrate that these methods are both legitimate and effective. Perhaps more important, however, is the spirit of rebellion shown us by Egyptian workers and students. We have seen that rebellion is correlated with certain demographic and economic characteristics shared by Egypt and the United States. Where unemployment is high, income inequality is large, and social media penetration is significant, the potential for rebellion is also high. This Middle Eastern profile fits the U.S. far more closely than our Western European counterparts. The OWS movement has highlighted this American reality as never before.

Workers must respond to employer decisions to close the plant, remove the machinery, and break the social contract. Worker occupations are the necessary and required response to them, just as OWS is to the financialization and corporatization of the American economy. They can be legally defended by way of eminent domain. Support from municipal councils and state legislatures are important ingredients, but worker mobilization is the indispensable first step. The economic crisis calls for such measures. Alliances must be established between public entities and authorities and the 99 percent (!) of the Americans who constitute the middle and working classes. A coalitional offensive needs to be mounted against the self-serving U.S. employer class that no longer upholds equity and fairness to its workers and employees.

Worker-managed factories and enterprises represent an attempt to bypass and even subvert the traditional capitalist firm as they experiment with workplace organization that avoids both the state socialist model of top-down controls and the capitalist hierarchical firms. They plant the seed in market economies that points to a third way of organizing work.

Eminent domain, however, should not be considered a revolutionary departure from traditional public policy that includes the powers to tax and spend, to regulate places of work environmentally, to zone for economic purposes, to apply rent control, and to protect workers and communities from health and safety hazards. The former depends on, and in turn complements, the latter.

With a novel approach to using eminent domain on behalf of workers for the clear benefit of economic development, social justice, and worker autonomy, we can reverse the trend of condemning an increasing number of communities to unemployment, a shrinking tax base, poverty with the concomitant rise of Medicaid and public assistance expenditures, and the continuing erosion of America's skilled labor force. How can communities continue to stand idly by while crucial employers, who have fed off the public trough and their loyal workers, often for decades, decide to get up and leave when the eminent domain procedure is available? Eminent domain is the viable mechanism that will place worker autonomy and worker rights at the center of the political debate in the defense against the continuing decline of decent jobs in America.

## Notes

1 Peter Ranis, "Argentina's Worker-Occupied Factories and Enterprises," *Socialism and Democracy*, 19, No. 3 (November 2005): 93-115 and "Factories without Bosses: Argentina's Experience with Worker-Run Enterprises," *Labor Studies in Working Class History of the Americas*, 3, No. 1 (Spring 2006): 11-23.
2 Peter Ranis, "Argentine Worker Cooperatives in Civil Society: A Challenge to Capital-Labor Relations," *Working USA: The Journal of Labor and Society,* 13, No. 1 (March 2010): 77-105.
3 Carl Davidson, *New Paths to Socialism* (Pittsburgh, PA: Changemaker Publications, 2011): 17-37; David Schweickart, *After Capitalism* (Lanham, MD: Rowman & Littlefield, 2011); Andrés Ruggeri, Las Empresas Recuperadas en la Argentina(Buenos Aires: Programa Facultad Abierta, Facultad de Filosofia y Letras de La Universidad de Buenos Aires, 2010); Marcelo Vieta, "The New Cooperativism," *Affinities: A Journal of Radical Theory, Culture and Action*, 4, No. 1 (2010): 1-8.
4 Judith D. Schwartz, "In Cleveland, Worker Co-Ops Look to a Spanish Model," Time (December 22, 2009).
5 Alan J. Robb, James H. Smith & Tom J. Webb, "Co-operative Capital: What It Is and Why Our World Needs It," paper for EURICSE Conference on Financial Cooperative Approaches to Local Development Through Sustainable Innovation, Trento, Italy, June 10-11, 2010: 8-9.

10

6 *New York Times*, October 26, 2011.
7 *New York Times*, May 2, 2011.
8 Robert E. Scott, "Heading South: U.S.-Mexico Trade and Job Displacement after NAFTA," Economic Policy Institute, May 3, 2011. Overall it has been estimated that since 2000, the U.S. has lost six million jobs and 50,000 enterprises have been shuttered.
9 James K. Galbraith, The Predator State: How Conservatives Abandoned the Free Market and Why Liberals Should Too(New York: *Free Press*, 2008).
10 Robert Skidelsky, Keynes: The Return of the Master: Why, Sixty Years after His Death, John Maynard Keynes Is the Most Important Economic Thinker for America(New York: Public Affairs Press, 2009). Income inequality in the U.S. has never been more skewed than in the present period. The U.S. Congressional Budget Office has shown that, from 1979 to 2007, average after-tax income grew 275 percent for the 1 percent of the population with the highest income. By contrast, the poorest fifth of the population's income rose by only 18 percent, while the three-fifths of the population in the middle-income sectors rose by 40 percent. The share of income for the top 1 percent climbed from 8 percent in 1979 to 17 percent in 2007. Those in the lowest fifth received 5 percent, down from 7 percent in 1979, and those in the middle three-fifth's share of income declined by 3 percent since 1979. See *The New York Times*, October 26, 2011.
11 Hector Palomino, et al., La Nueva Dinámica de las Relaciones Laborales en la Argentina (Buenos Aires: Jorge Baudino Ediciones, 2010): 36.
12 Ranis (2005): 100-105.
13 Palomino (2010): 29.
14 Ranis (2010): 89.
15 Julián Rebon, Desobedeciendo el Desempleo (Buenos Aires: Ediciones Picaso/La Rosa Blindada, 2004).
16 Ruggeri (2010).
17 Ibid., 7, 37.
18 Ibid., 18-19.
19 Ibid., 69-70.
20 Ibid., 44-46, 52, 54.
21 Ibid., 77-79.
22 Ranis (2010).
23 For example, there are approximately 7,400 cooperative credit unions servicing 93,000,000 people in the U.S. Worldwide, one billion people are associated with cooperatives.
24 Peter Ranis, "Eminent Domain: Unused Tool for American Labor," Working USA: *The Journal of Labor and Society*, 10, No. 2 (June 2007): 193-208.
25 David Gutknecht, "Thinking Outside the Coop," *Cooperative Grocer*, #136 (May-June, 2008): 5. Robb, Smith and Webb argue similarly, "Cooperatives, rather than being forced to invest their savings in obscure financial instruments that offend their values and finance investor capital endeavors in distant places, will be able to see their savings used to meet needs closer to home" (16).
26 *The New York Times*, March 1, 2011.
27 Peter Ranis, "Worker-Run U.S. Factories and Enterprises: The Example of Argentine Cooperatives," In Emily Kawano, ed. Solidarity Economy: Building Alternatives for People and Planet (Amherst, MA., Center for Popular Economics, 2009), 115-123.
28 Kari Lydersen, Revolt on Goose Island: The Chicago Factory Takeover and what it Says About the Economic Crisis (New York: Melville House, 2009) and Ranis, 2009.
29 Steven Greenhouse, The Big Squeeze: Tough Times for the American Worker (New York: Alfred A. Knopf, 2008).

*Peter Ranis is professor emeritus in the Ph.D. Program in Political Science at the Graduate Center, CUNY. He is the author of numerous books and articles and is an activist member of his union-the Professional Staff Congress of CUNY. He can be reached at ranis@ york.cuny.edu.*

# Global Rebellion: The Coming Chaos?

## Global Elites are Confused, Reactive, and Sinking into a Quagmire of Their Own Making

### By William I. Robinson

As the crisis of global capitalism spirals out of control, the powers that be in the global system appear to be adrift and unable to proposal viable solutions. From the slaughter of dozens of young protesters by the army in Egypt to the brutal repression of the Occupy movement in the United States, and the water cannons brandished by the militarized police in Chile against students and workers, states and ruling classes are unable are to hold back the tide of worldwide popular rebellion and must resort to ever more generalized repression.

Simply put, the immense structural inequalities of the global political economy can no longer be contained through consensual mechanisms of social control. The ruling classes have lost legitimacy; we are witnessing a breakdown of ruling-class hegemony on a world scale.

To understand what is happening in this second decade of the new century we need to see the big picture in historic and structural context. Global elites had hoped and expected that the "Great Depression" that began with the mortgage crisis and the collapse of the global financial system in 2008 would be a cyclical downturn that could be resolved through state-sponsored bailouts and stimulus packages. But it has become clear that this is a structural crisis. Cyclical crises are on-going episodes in the capitalist system, occurring about once a decade and usually last 18 months to two years. There were world recessions in the early 1980s, the early 1990s, and the early 21st century.

### Structural Crises and Cyclical Crisis

Structural crises are deeper; their resolution requires a fundamental restructuring of the system. Earlier world structural crises of the 1890s, the 1930s and the 1970s were resolved through a reorganization of the system that produced new models of capitalism. "Resolved" does not mean that the problems faced by a majority of humanity under capitalism were resolved but that the reorganization of the capitalist system in each case overcame the constraints to a resumption of capital accumulation on a world scale. The crisis of the 1890s was resolved in the cores of world capitalism through the export of capital and a new round of imperialist expansion. The Great Depression of the 1930s was resolved through the turn to variants of social democracy in both the North and the South - welfare, populist, or developmentalist capitalism that involved redistribution, the creation of public sectors, and state regulation of the market.

## Globalization and the current structural crisis

To understand the current conjuncture we need to go back to the 1970s. The globalization stage of world capitalism we are now in itself evolved out the response of distinct agents to these previous episodes of crisis, in particular, to the 1970s crisis of social democracy, or more technically stated, of Fordism-Keynesianism, or of redistributive capitalism. In the wake of that crisis capital went global as a strategy of the emergent Transnational Capitalist Class and its political representatives to reconstitute its class power by breaking free of nation-state constraints to accumulation. These constraints - the so-called "class compromise" - had been imposed on capital through decades of mass struggles around the world by nationally-contained popular and working classes. During the 1980s and 1990s, however, globally-oriented elites captured state power in most countries around the world and utilized that power to push capitalist globalization through the neo-liberal model.

## Revolution in Information Technology

Globalization and neo-liberal policies opened up vast new opportunities for transnational accumulation in the 1980s and 1990s. The revolution in computer and information technology and other technological advances helped emergent transnational capital to achieve major gains in productivity and to restructure, "flexibilize," and shed labor worldwide. This, in turn, undercut wages and the social wage and facilitated a transfer of income to capital and to high consumption sectors around the world that provided new market segments fueling growth. In sum, globalization made possible a major extensive and intensive expansion of the system and unleashed a frenzied new round of accumulation worldwide that offset the 1970s crisis of declining profits and investment opportunities.

However, the neo-liberal model has also resulted in an unprecedented worldwide social polarization. Fierce social and class struggles worldwide were able in the 20th century to impose a measure of social control over capital. Popular classes, to varying degrees, were able to force the system to link what we call social reproduction to capital accumulation. What has taken place through globalization is the severing of the logic of accumulation from that of social reproduction, resulting in an unprecedented growth of social inequality and intensified crises of survival for billions of people around the world.

The pauperizing effects unleashed by globalization have generated social conflicts and political crises that the system is now finding more and more difficult to contain. The slogan "we are the 99 per cent" grows out of the reality that global inequalities and pauperization have intensified enormously since capitalist globalization took off in the 1980s. Broad swaths of humanity have experienced absolute downward mobility in recent decades. Even the IMF was forced to admit in a 2000 report that "in recent decades, nearly one-fifth of the world's population has regressed. This is arguably one of the greatest economic failures of the 20th century".

Global social polarization intensifies the chronic problem of over-accumulation. This refers to the concentration of wealth in fewer and fewer hands, so that the global market is unable to absorb world output and the system stagnates. Transnational capitalists find it more and more difficult to unload their bloated and expanding mass of surplus - they can't find outlets to invest their money in order to generate new profits; hence the system enters into recession or worse. In recent years, the Transnational Capitalist Class has turned to militarized accumulation, to wild financial speculation, and to the raiding or sacking of public finance to sustain profit-making in the face of over-accumulation.

## Great Recession as Turning Point

While transnational capital's offensive against the global working and popular classes dates back to the crisis of the 1970s and has grown in intensity ever since, the Great Recession of 2008 was in several respects a major turning point. In particular, as the crisis spread it generated the conditions for new rounds of brutal austerity worldwide, greater flexibilization of labor, steeply rising under and unemployment, and so on. Transnational finance capital and its political agents utilized the global crisis to impose brutal austerity and attempting to dismantle what is left of welfare systems and social states in Europe, North America, and elsewhere, to squeeze more value out of labor, directly through more intensified exploitation and indirectly through state finances. Social and political conflict has escalated around the world in the wake of 2008.

Nonetheless, the system has been unable to recover; it is sinking deeper into chaos. Global elites cannot manage the explosive contradictions. Is the neo-liberal model of capitalism entering a terminal stage? It is crucial to understand that neo-liberalism is but one model of global capitalism; to say that neo-liberalism may be in terminal crisis is not to say that global capitalism is in terminal crisis. Is it possible that the system will respond to crisis and mass rebellion through a new restructuring that leads to some different model of world capitalism—perhaps a global Keynesianism involving transnational redistribution and transnational regulation of finance capital? Will rebellious forces from below be co-opted into some new reformed capitalist order?

Or are we headed towards a systemic crisis? A systemic crisis is one in which the solution involves the end of the system itself, either through its super-session and the creation of an entirely new system, or more ominously the collapse of the system. Whether or not a structural cri-sis becomes systemic depends on how distinct social and class forces respond—to the political projects they put forward and as well as to factors of contingency that cannot be predicted in advance, and to ob-jective conditions. It is impossible at this time to predict the outcome of the crisis. However, a few things are clear in the current world con-juncture.

The current moment First, this crisis shares a number of aspects with earlier structural crises of the 1930s and the 1970s, but there are also several features unique to the present:

The system is fast reaching the ecological limits of its reproduction. We face the real specter of resource depletion and environmental catastro-phes that threaten a system collapse.

The magnitude of the means of violence and social control is unprec-edented. Computerized wars, drones, bunker-buster bombs, star wars, and so forth, have changed the face of warfare. Warfare has become normalized and sanitized for those not directly at the receiving end of armed aggression. Also unprecedented is the concentration of control over the mass media, the production of symbols, images and messages in the hands of transnational capital. We have arrived at the society of panoptical surveillance and Orwellian thought control.

## Reaching the Limits

We are reaching the limits to the extensive expansion of capitalism, in the sense that there are no longer any new territories of significance that can be integrated into world capitalism. De-ruralization is now well-advanced, and the commodification of the countryside and of pre- and non-capitalist spaces has intensified, that is, converted in hot-house fashion into spaces of capital, so that intensive expansion is reaching depths never before seen. Like riding a bicycle, the capitalist system needs to continuously expand or else it collapses. Where can the system now expand?

There is the rise of a vast surplus population inhabiting a planet of slums, alienated from the productive economy, thrown into the margins, and subject to sophisticated systems of social control and to crises of survival—to a mortal cycle of dispossession-exploitation-exclusion. This raises in new ways the dangers of a 21st-century fascism and new episodes of genocide to contain the mass of surplus humanity and their real or potential rebellion.

There is a disjuncture between a globalizing economy and a nation-state based system of political authority. Transnational state apparatuses are incipient and have not been able to play the role of what social scientists refer to as a "hegemon", or a leading nation-state that has enough power and authority to organize and stabilize the system. Nation-states cannot control the howling gales of a runaway global economy; states face expanding crises of political legitimacy.

## Global Elites at a Loss

Second, global elites are unable to come up with solutions. They appear to be politically bankrupt and impotent to steer the course of events unfolding before them. They have exhibited bickering and division at the G-8, G-20 and other forums, seemingly paralyzed, and certainly unwilling to challenge the power and prerogative of transnational finance capital, the hegemonic fraction of capital on a world scale, and the most rapacious and destabilizing fraction. While national and transnational state apparatuses fail to intervene to impose regulations on global finance capital, they have intervened to impose the costs of the crisis on labor. The budgetary and fiscal crises that supposedly justify spending cuts and austerity are contrived. They are a consequence of the unwillingness or inability of states to challenge capital and their disposition to transfer the burden of the crisis to working and popular classes.

Third, there will be no quick outcome of the mounting global chaos. We are in for a period of major conflicts and great upheavals. As I mentioned above, one danger is a neo-fascist response to contain the crisis. We are facing a war of capital against all. Three sectors of transnational capital in particular stand out as the most aggressive and prone to seek neo-fascist political arrangements to force forward accumulation as this crisis continues: speculative financial capital, the military-industrial-security complex, and the extractive and energy sector. Capital accumulation in the military-industrial-security complex depends on endless conflicts and war, including the so-called wars on terrorism and on drugs, as well as on the militarization of social control. Transnational finance capital depends on taking control of state finances and imposing debt and austerity on the masses, which in turn can only be achieved through escalating repression. And extractive industries depend on new rounds of violent dispossession and environmental degradation around the world.

Fourth, popular forces worldwide have moved quicker than anyone could imagine from the defensive to the offensive. The initiative clearly passed this year, 2011, from the transnational elite to popular forces from below. The juggernaut of capitalist globalization in the 1980s and 1990s had reverted the correlation of social and class forces worldwide in favor of transnational capital. Although resistance continued around the world, popular forces from below found themselves disoriented and fragmented in those decades, pushed on to the defensive in the heyday of neo-liberalism. Then the events of September 11, 2001, allowed the transnational elite, under the leadership of the US state, to sustain its offensive by militarizing world politics and extending systems of repressive social control in the name of "combating terrorism".

Now all this has changed. The global revolt underway has shifted the whole political landscape and the terms of the discourse. Global elites are confused, reactive, and sinking into the quagmire of their own making. It is noteworthy that those struggling around the world have been shown a strong sense of solidarity and are in communications across whole continents. Just as the Egyptian uprising inspired the US Occupy movement, the latter has been an inspiration for a new round of mass struggle in Egypt. What remains is to extend transnational coordination and move towards transnationally-coordinated programs. On the other hand, the "empire of global capital" is definitely not a "paper tiger". As global elites regroup and assess the new conjuncture and the threat of mass global revolution, they will - and have already begun to - organize coordinated mass repression, new wars and interventions, and mechanisms and projects of co-optation in their efforts to restore hegemony.

In my view, the only viable solution to the crisis of global capitalism is a massive redistribution of wealth and power downward towards the poor majority of humanity along the lines of a 21st-century democratic socialism in which humanity is no longer at war with itself and with nature.

© 2011 William I. Robinson

*William I. Robinson is a Professor of Sociology, Global Studies, and Latin American Studies, University of California at Santa Barbara. His latest book is Latin America and Global Capitalism.*

# The Growing Split at the Top Is an Opportunity for the Progressive Majority in 2012

## By Randy Shannon and Carl Davidson

From the Great Depression of 1929 to the Great Recession of 2007 US capitalism has maintained social stability and the consent of the governed by sustaining the "American Dream."

"Indeed, expanding opportunity and increasing prosperity through broad-based growth are at the core of the American Dream that has stitched our country together through good times and bad."(1)

Now global capitalism is experiencing a deep structural crisis that its leaders appear unable to resolve. Einstein's dictum that "The significant problems we face today cannot be solved at the same level of thinking we were at when we created them" remains valid. Finance capital has failed to solve the financial, economic, and social crisis in the interests of society. The "American Dream" is at risk.

There is a growing divergence among financial elites over the path forward. The ebb and flow of this sharpening division continues to be reflected in US Government policy. The search for a solution to the crisis offers an important opportunity to strengthen the voice of the progressive majority, especially in the context of the 2012 elections. The U.S left is finding a more receptive public for its sorely needed new thinking.

At the beginning of the crisis, the elites unified to save their insolvent banks and maintain political power. As the Obama administration assumed office, the Goldman Sachs gang maintained its powerful positions in the Federal Reserve, the US Treasury and other government agencies. The Fed defended the bondholders of the insolvent banks by exchanging US treasuries for their worthless mortgage backed securities. The Treasury subordinated public interest to private interests, and empowered the worst of capitalism by bailing out the criminal bankers.

The Obama campaign won the election, but once in office had to share power with the Goldman Sachs gang, the entrenched military industry, and the neoliberal Democrats represented by Chief of Staff Rahm Emmanuel. This uneasy coalition struggled to implement health care reform and an economic stimulus to create jobs with a majority of Republicans and Blue Dog Democrats in Congress. These compromised achievements failed to reverse the economic collapse.

Chronic high unemployment, growing homelessness and hunger, a massive reduction in the wealth of working people, along with policy decisions clearly in service to members of this coalition, undermined public support for the Obama administration. Obama was also forced to negotiate the terms of ending the war with the entrenched powers in the military. These concessions weakened the progressive forces at the base of the governing coalition.

## 2010 Right Wing Offensive

The failure of the Obama administration to meet expectations of a quick end to the economic decline left the electorate disillusioned in 2010. Frustrated voters were assaulted by a Republican juggernaut of lies and distortions funded by unlimited corporate financing thanks to the Supreme Court's Citizen United decision. As a result, right wing Republicans gained control of Congress and many state governments.

The 2010 election forced the Obama administration into a more defensive posture. The White House brought William Daley in as chief of staff as an opening to conservative business interests. While the President was unable to move new legislation, the Democratic Senate majority and the threat of Presidential veto blocked the right wing agenda. The right wing tried to force the White House to accept an austere budget by threatening to cut off government funding and refusing to raise the debt ceiling. The President maneuvered to prevent the new Republican majority from gutting Social Security and Medicare and defunding critical government agencies.

In a number of states the new Republican majorities began to implement the neoliberal agenda with a vengeance. These neoliberal policies centered on the destruction of unions and social programs, the corporate takeover of government responsibilities, and deregulation of corporate activities. Some 800 'model' bills designed by the American Legislative Exchange Council (ALEC), a corporate funded think tank, were introduced in these states. (2) These programs strip workers of basic rights, privatize education and health care and eliminate environmental protections under the "Right to Work" rubric. The use of prison labor for private profit was legalized; stricter sentencing laws were passed; and the probation system was privatized. A series of vicious anti-immigrant laws, voter restrictions, and laws to deprive women of basic human rights were passed in these states.

## Grassroots Resistance Grows

First in Wisconsin and then Ohio and other states, elements of this policy met with vigorous resistance by working people. The resistance has jelled into broad democratic movements that gathered a million signatures in Wisconsin to recall the far right Governor and placed a referendum on the ballot in Ohio that overwhelmingly defeated the Republican's new anti-union legislation.

Social resistance to neoliberal policies is spreading and solidifying. The powerful resistance to the reactionary Republican attack on workers in Wisconsin and in Ohio has energized the union movement and brought hundreds of thousands into the political struggle. The Occupy Wall Street movement has shattered the neoliberal theme of austerity and "less government equals more jobs." Occupy has raised the issue of class division within the "American Dream" by showing that the greed of the super-rich oppresses the majority 99%. The union-led resistance and the Occupy movement reflect an important shift in public consciousness.

The resistance of the masses of Europeans and the people of North Africa and the Middle East to the neoliberal policy of war and austerity has forced their governments to maneuver or compromise. In Italy and Greece, where austerity policies are in full force and the rate of economic decline is unprecedented, banker appointed technocrats pushed out popularly elected governments. Austerity policies in Spain, Portugal and Ireland have resulted in massive unemployment and social dislocation with voters punishing the parties that agreed to the policy. Arab Spring has resulted in the overthrow of many autocratic regimes that served the interests of multi-national corporations and starved their people.

## Dynamics of Austerity

The US continues to suffer from a jobless recovery in which millions are counted out of the labor force while corporate profits soar. Austerity increases short-term profits by curtailing the ability of the working class to fight for sustainable wages and working conditions. Austerity takes tax moneys from social needs such as jobs, healthcare and infrastructure and channels funds to bank bondholders and other corporate subsidies. This forces working people to subsidize the social wage by taking on the expense of crucial social services from childcare to elderly care.

The austerity policy reflects the interests of the most reactionary sector of capital from the military-energy industrial complex to the Wall Street banks. Austerity decreases personal income, consumption, and tax remissions by pushing more people into low wage jobs and poverty. Austerity accelerates the deflationary trend of falling values and slowing economic activity. This results in a new economic crisis that provides the wealthy 1% the opportunity to accumulate vast social wealth at a discount. At the same time it raises social tensions and destabilizes the political consensus.

## Caution on Austerity

On January 20, 2012, the leaders of the International Monetary Fund, the World Bank, the World Trade Organization and eight other multilateral and regional institutions issued a joint statement warning that the world faced "significant and urgent challenges." The statement warned that austerity threatens "decelerating global growth and rising uncertainty; high unemployment, especially youth unemployment..." The global financial elite represented by the IMF warned that governments should "manage fiscal consolidation to promote rather than reduce prospects for growth and employment." (3)

Only a week earlier the Obama Administration began to distance itself from the forces supporting neoliberal austerity policies. It removed Chief of Staff Daley, a confidant of Republican business leaders, and replaced him with Jacob Lew, a member of the Hamilton Project. The Hamilton Project proposes to delay austerity until after a recovery. "As part of this strategy to shift focus to long run prosperity, the United States should begin to confront the deficit as soon as the economic recovery has gained sufficient momentum." (4) The Hamilton Project is a group of financiers founded by Robert Rubin that develops policies that maintain their social and political dominance in the United States.

Federal Reserve chairman Bernanke in a recent press appearance stated that "we need to be thinking about ways to provide further stimulus if we don't get improvement in the pace of recovery and a normalization of inflation." 'Normalization of inflation' is "Fedspeak" for stopping the deflationary trend, the downward spiral in value of wages and property. *The New York Times* quoted Bernanke's recent testimony before Congress: "I think it would repay your efforts to remove some of the barriers to a recovery in housing." According to the *Times,* "Mr. Bernanke repeated his familiar caution that Congress should not cut spending or raise taxes too quickly, because doing so could undermine the economic recovery..."

These leading financial elites' criticism of neoliberal austerity policy reflect two central concerns. First, deeper austerity will cause a deeper economic crisis that could threaten capitalism's survival. Second, the social pressure against austerity could displace the financial elite from political power. The forces opposing austerity are also trying to isolate and weaken the neoliberals. For example, the Consumer Financial Protection Act shepherded through Congress by Elizabeth Warren reduces the freedom of action of the Wall Street bankers. In addition, multi-billion dollar lawsuits against the criminal mortgage bankers are moving forward.

## 2012 Battleground

Election year 2012 opens on a new juncture in the struggle over the outcome of this crisis of capitalism. The global, national and local struggle of working people to push back the onslaught of predatory capitalism is growing. It is clear that a US Presidential election alone will not resolve this deep crisis. But a mass movement will use all of the tools available to fight the neoliberal policy of war and austerity. In this light, the defeat of the reactionary core in the Republican Party is part and parcel of building the momentum of the growing resistance of the working people.

The defeat of the reactionary coalition of Tea Party, racists, nationalists, militarists, speculators, and right wing billionaires and hedge fund owners is a key task that 2012 presents the working class and its allies in the progressive majority. Mass demonstrations and occupations held in conjunction with voter registration drives and marches on the polls during the primaries and in November will widen the split within the governing financial elite.

Central to broadening this struggle is the fight for unity against the racist, sexist and anti-immigrant laws on the state level. The racist rhetoric in the Republican presidential campaign combined with the attack on voting rights and immigrants, especially in the South, is designed to divide and demobilize white voters and intimidate black voters. An urgent struggle against the new state laws that deny the franchise to youth, minorities and the elderly with new voter restrictions can strengthen the progressive coalition by making common cause the defense of basic democratic rights.

The financiers around President Obama who oppose austerity want to expand financialization with more credit, currency devaluation and inflation, also known as "kicking the can down the road." Their stimulus policy consists of creating more low interest credit and bailouts for the banks. More financialization will delay, but not solve, the economic crisis. The electoral campaigns in the primaries and the general election should resound with the demand to not only end the policy of austerity, but to replace it with direct investment in the infrastructure, taxes on the wealthy and Wall Street transactions to fund a jobs program, prosecution of the criminal bankers, restitution for defrauded homeowners, and a halt to home foreclosures. The progressive program can be a model for how government can serve the people and their communities.

A real solution to the economic crisis starts with the Congressional Progressive Caucus People's Budget and a program of Full Employment, Medicare for All and Student Debt Forgiveness. These are the framework for real economic expansion and are the bottom line for the progressive majority. The progressive majority should develop a campaign to rehabilitate the social wage and expose its detractors in order to counter the ideological basis for austerity. As the Occupy movement shows, reclaiming the interpretation of the American Dream from the corporate media in order to reflect the immediate reality of the people is the basis to build broad political action.

## The US Left – Pulling Together

The slow pace of independent political efforts by labor and the progressive majority during the 2010 election reflected, in part, the weaknesses of the left. The most effective role of the left today is to work with the progressive majority to defeat the neoliberal policies of austerity. The upsurge of struggle to turn back the reactionary onslaught of the Republican right is the context for building unity among the many sectors. The left must work to consciously build unity of African Americans, Latinos, Asian/Pacific Islanders and Native Americans, youth, seniors, women and men, lesbian and gay and immigrant peoples.

The ebb and flow of the struggle within the Obama administration continues to require on the part of the left a high level of tactical flexibility and the ability to distinguish the parts from the whole in the political sphere. Frustration at the failures of the Obama coalition to reverse decades of entrenchment by the neoliberal bloc feeds the view that there is no difference at the top. The key to this stage of struggle is to build broad popular unity and mass action to defeat austerity. This will isolate the reactionary sectors of capital and provide space for building a new ruling coalition that to some degree includes the progressive majority.

The coming period will see an intense struggle to defend the living standards of the working class, to end the war in Afghanistan and prevent new wars, and to address the crisis of global warming. The neoliberal assault on the living standard and social cohesion of the working class should be answered by growing dialogue and cooperation among the left, including efforts at joint action and programmatic unity. The politically conscious left in the US is larger, perhaps many times larger than the organized left. Common projects of socialist organizations would become a magnet for the majority on the left who would align with a culturally and politically vibrant and growing socialist movement. Such a socialist movement with a public face would tap into the progressive vision of the majority of American youth today who view socialism as preferable to capitalism and who demand new thinking for peaceful and prosperous future.

## Footnotes:

1. The Hamilton Project Strategy Paper April 2010, "From Recession to Recovery to Renewal: An Economic Strategy to Achieve Broadly Shared Growth"
2. ALEC is the American Legislative Exchange Council. Through the corporate-funded American Legislative Exchange Council, global corporations and state politicians vote behind closed doors to try to rewrite state laws that govern your rights. http://alecexposed.org/wiki/ALEC_Exposed
3. "IMF Warns of Threat to Global Economies Posed by Austerity Drives" The Guardian 01/19/2012
4. See (1)

*Randy Shannon is a national committee member of CCDS. Carl Davidson is a national co-chair of CCDS. They both reside and organize in Beaver County, near Pittsburgh in Western Pennsylvania*

# Obama and the Left

## By Mark Solomon

There is arguably no issue on the left as bitterly contentious as the presidency of Barack Obama and how to approach his campaign for reelection this year. (The left, I realize, is an imprecise category. Here, we speak of a broad progressive community in struggle for change. While acknowledging that there are significant differences among various forces on the left, for purposes of discussion we nevertheless conjoin socialists, independent progressives, and left-of center Democratic party liberals.)

The disillusionment and disappointment with Obama in some quarters on the left ranged from reasoned criticism to borderline hysteria. The President has been criticized for pursuing a foreign policy that largely remains anchored upon traditional imperial priorities and projection of military might. Within that inherited framework of imperial pursuit, he has authorized widespread use of updated killing technologies like non-defensive drone attacks, has failed to close Guantanamo, has maintained huge levels of military spending, has signed the National Defense Appropriations Act that among other things enables indefinite detention without trial of "terrorism suspects," including US citizens, has not prosecuted the Bush regime architects of torture, etc. He has also tamped down standard opposition to Israeli settlement expansion on the West Bank (thus undermining lingering hope for a two-state arrangement), has resisted a global ban on cluster bombs, has zealously rounded up non-documented immigrants, has vigorously pursued government secrecy, etc.

### Serious Criticism, Taken Seriously

Such serious criticism deserves careful consideration. Less so, sweeping, largely unsubstantiated claims based not on analysis, but on subjective feelings of betrayal. One Massachusetts activist recently wrote: "He has stabbed nearly every constituency in his coalition in the back from labor to civil rights to the environmentalists." That was topped by a group of predominantly white demonstrators who recently appeared at an Obama fundraiser at the Apollo Theater in Harlem – attacking the President for everything from killing family farms to allegedly preventing access to emergency contraception to delisting wolves as a federal protected species.

*Street heat in Kentucky, with CCDS's Janet Tucker in the center*

Whether measured or unrestrained, both types of criticism suffer from two basic flaws. They fail to probe systemic and institutional structures that both shape and impact the relationship between the presidency and those structures. That is a major problem on the left. By failing to closely examine the role and function of historically evolved and deeply embedded structures such as the military-industrial complex and a globalized and financialized economy (with a major segment of corporate capital buying political power to suppress working class interests and throttle democracy) the left cannot readily locate the prime sources of destructive power. Thus, the left is hindered in developing appropriate strategies (including mass educational efforts) to contest those structures as well as in seeking fissures in ruling circles that open opportunities for vital, effective coalitions.

## The One-Dimensional Flaw

The second major flaw is a one-dimensional view of the Obama White House that fails to attain needed balance and thus fails to grasp the contradictory nature of the President's outlook. That weakness denies the progressive community the opportunity to act upon what is positive, what advances progress; what contributes to building political cooperation among diverse forces; what is negative and must be fought. That is especially essential if there is to be serious engagement in the electoral arena.

Especially in electoral politics where for the foreseeable future a predominant two-party "winner take all" system will persist, it's vital to assess where progressive gains can be made within the limits of that system, where and how mass political awareness can be advanced, where effective coalitions can be built, which tactics would hold favorable prospects for advancing political independence, around which candidates and issues can grass roots progressive movements grow, and vitally, which political forces on the right must urgently be defeated, even if that requires tactical support of candidates whose views may not fully calibrate the positions of progressive activists. One thing is certain in US politics: without considering the balance of political forces, holding to an absolute moral high ground, no matter how objectively justified, is a prescription for irrelevance and isolation.

Barack Obama, from the very start of his political career was never a critic of the country's systemic failures (even though he was intellectually aware of left critiques of the system). On the contrary, he was (and is) a skilled, pragmatic politician embedded in the system dominated by corporate capital – sincerely advocating moderate reforms shorn of direct confrontation with corporate and military power. In addressing the Deerfield Forum in January 2009, we noted:

"Obama's ideas and policies were always at the liberal center of the political spectrum," also noting his "penchant for pragmatic compromises and straddling a line through the center...Running for President, he stood above race and class. He avoided speaking in ideological terms and even when calling for the right to health care, or to organize unions, or to be protected against thieving mortgage lenders – he spoke of collective will and building community across ideological lines. Such a politics of 'unity' suggested that what is wrong with politics is the way it is conducted, rather than its service to corporate wealth and military power."

**Clouded Vision**

While grasping a vision of reform—the vision itself was clouded by a latent sense of comfort with and acceptance of the world of finance capital. More important, his commitment to progress is circumscribed by a weighty awareness of the power of big capital, and its ability to do devastating damage to those in the political arena that breach the political boundaries set by that power.

Ron Suskind's study of the early days of the Obama administration provides insight into the President's ideological and political limitations –

and the limits placed upon him. (It also reveals the fissures that open opportunities to press Obama to the left-of-center.) In the lame duck days between Obama's election and his ascension to the Oval Office, battle lines were forming on the pressing issue of the moment – the massive collapse of the financial system. Two clearly defined currents were emerging: an "A team" that advocated quick, highly prioritized re-regulation of Wall Street, including temporary nationalization of collapsing banks. That group included Robert Reich, Laura Tyson, Austan Goolsbee, Robert Wolf—with graybeard John Volcker hovering. A "B Team" squired by Robert Rubin with strong ties to behemoth Goldman Sachs, contested that group. The members are now household names: Lawrence Summers, Ben Bernanke, Timothy Geithner and lesser lights.

Obama initially was inclined to follow the counsel of the "A Team." However, the Rubin group warned that decisive action to re-regulate and partially nationalize would be met with fierce, even destructive resistance. They warned Obama that in following the advice of Reich and the others, he would provoke total Wall Street intransigence, including cutoff of what remained of the credit structure, bringing the economy to its knees. The multi-billion dollar bailout would have to go forward without conditions or constraints. Summers and Geithner invoked a variant of the Hippocratic oath: "First, Do No Harm." That is: no harm to finance capital – adding that nothing should impede the return to stability of that system.

Obama was confronted with the seemingly boundless institutional power of Wall Street. Despite a personal inclination to adopt a fairly clearcut reform, he opted to back the bailout without conditions. Getting an unambiguous signal from the financial system, Obama installed Summers, Geithner, Bernanke and company to take charge of the government role in returning Wall Street to "stability." The institutional power of the financial system was obtusely affirmed when as President, Obama instructed Geithner to "dissolve" Citigroup. Geithner, often described as "Wall Streets' man in the White House," ignored the president. Instead, Treasury converted its preferred shares in Citigroup into riskier common stock, bailing it out for the third time and preserving the bank's management, its $2 trillion balance sheet, and its coveted status as too big to fail threat to the global economy. (Geither's recent admission that he won't be asked to stay in a second Obama administration is encouraging.)

The installation of the Summers, Geithner, Bernanke group was the first sign for disappointed progressives that the change advocated by the presidential candidate would not constitute a challenge to, or departure from, the dominant influence of the financial system.

## Reform and the Balance of Power

The major struggle over universal health care in the new administration defined the parameters—and the limits of reform in the face of present power arrangements. The new President had signaled his understanding that single payer was the only way to fully control costs while providing health care to all without limit. But he added that single payer would only have been possible if "the nation was starting from scratch." He was faced with a powerful private insurance industry poised to torpedo any breakthrough on health care that included a public option – much less single payer. Many on the left faulted Obama for failing to at least confront Congress, much of it in the pocket of the industry, with a strong starting position – at least a public option. The end result: at long last – health care legislation that finally brought reforms around the edges of the insurance industry – while also handing it a windfall in the form of individual mandates to buy private insurance.

With all that, a nagging crisis of unemployment and stirring protest, wrought fissures within corporate capital. Some elements were increasingly repelled by the reckless and socially dangerous right wing within their ranks that abnegated any traditional responsibility for "social peace" through selective concessions to working and middle classes. The principal Wall Street protectors of the financial system tied to the Administration now advocated stimulus packages (coupled with tax cuts) to spur jobs in the face of a deep crisis and a threat from the right. That new current paralleled an emerging trend in severely crisis-ridden European Union to rein in the frenetic drive to impose austerity on weak on states drowning in sovereign debt. European Union member agencies are now advocating investment in jobs and growth to forestall a total collapse.

## The Hamilton Project

A group within the capitalist establishment has emerged largely from the Hamilton Project of the Brookings Institution to engage the issues of low incomes, failing education, economic stagnation, etc. Brookings itself is a centrist elite institution with a range of sponsors and participants from academia and other professions, high finance, global businesses and high technology.

Hamilton's economic program parallels Obama's prescriptions for tackling the crisis: heavy investment in education and retraining to halt, if not reverse erosion of stable working class employment and stagnating incomes; large investment in research and development along with infrastructure investment in green technologies and manufacturing; long-term debt reduction while the government expands "high value" investment in education and upgrade of infrastructure. To the extent that the

Hamilton Project group advocates the commitment of large resources to generate employment, improve education, convert to a green economy and rehabilitate the country's rotting infrastructure, progressives can usefully support elements of Obama's re-election program that have progressive elements.

Given the class forces that are represented by the Hamilton Project, it is perhaps no surprise that its program says nothing about workers' rights and defense of unions and collective bargaining, about the Employee Free Choice Act, about raising minimum wages, about the rights of the undocumented, etc. There is nothing about large-scale efforts to quickly generate jobs through New Deal WPA type programs, nothing about progressive taxation and ending the Bush tax cuts for the super rich, and of course, nothing about reducing military spending, closing overseas bases and ending wars. (That also to a great extent reflects the limitations and failures of the Obama Administration).

Pressure for those policies will have to come from other quarters. In some critical areas Obama has begun to breach the limits of the Hamilton program. His striking declaration in his State of the Union address: "the defining issue of our time is income inequality," is an indisputable reflection of the impact of OWS and of those who rallied to the call for mobilizing "the 99 percent." Recent victories for progressives in stopping (for the time being) the Keystone XL pipeline, shelving Internet censorship, extending jobless benefits, fending off attacks on "day after" contraception– affirm the power of grass roots activism to move the Administration, however haltingly, to the left. Most important, OWS and a resurgent labor movement (beginning to slowly grow again) and a constellation of progressive forces have provided the firepower to move Obama away from seeking accommodation with rigid, obstructionist Republicans and toward defiantly demanding action on jobs, education, foreclosure relief, ending the Bush super rich tax cuts as well as breaking the log jam on executive appointments.

For some on the left this perceptible shift in direction is merely peripheral and does not alter their often bitterly negative assessment of Obama. However, failure to see changes in a progressive direction, no matter how modest, seriously underestimates leftward moving public consciousness and the impact of growing demonstrative action – negating significant opportunities for substantive change in a crucial election cycle.

## Centrists Vacillate by Their Nature

Of course, given the centrist character of the Administration and the power of entrenched institutions symbolized by Wall Street and the Pentagon, retreats, vacillation and compromises by the Obama administration are to be anticipated—mandating stronger countervailing efforts by OWS and the broad range of progressive movements.

Given the contradictory nature of the Administration, it is not surprising that shelving of the Keystone XL pipeline is accompanied by authorization for more offshore oil drilling and natural gas fracturing; path breaking creation of a Justice Department fraud unit to investigate (and perhaps to finally jail) fraudulent bank mortgage practices is matched by a proposed government settlement with the big banks that in the words of Van Jones pays "a tiny fraction of what is needed for blanket immunity from future lawsuits." (The proposed settlement would have the banks pay only $20 billion when there is $700 billion in underwater mortgages. In a late development it appears that banks will remain exposed to a variety of serious charges, a victory for states attorneys general). After Draconian roundups of immigrants, the Administration has narrowed its dragnet to those with criminal records. But hundreds of thousands have already been deported and many still await deportation and family breakup. Obama out-maneuvered the Republicans to continue "middle class" tax cuts. But that came at the cost of raiding the Social Security fund. Programs to generate jobs, especially in the energy sector, have been coupled with new tax breaks for businesses.

It's vital for progressives to recognize the advances for economic and social justice under Obama in recent weeks and months (including decisive action by the new Consumer Financial Protection Bureau). That should constitute encouragement and a goad to continue to build grass roots pressure to counter the hegemonic influence of corporate capital and the Pentagon. It's equally important to recognize and fight Administration retreats and concessions to the right. An election cycle, a period of broad public engagement in political issues, is a propitious political moment to advance a progressive program. The Congressional Progressive Caucus and others have spelled out demands from major bank reform to extensive job creation, to progressive taxation including a derivatives and speculation tax, from controlling escalating student loans to green energy, to protecting Social Security and Medicare to extending health care reform to ending the wars and spending military funds for human needs.

Perhaps the most institutionally rooted and intractable region of governing power is the military-industrial complex abetted by the political establishment – stretching from the Pentagon to military bases and industries with more than 33 million people dependent upon it. For more than a century-and-a-half at least, the existence of the military as the armed enforcer of empire has been a virtually unquestioned aspect of the country's political system. No Administration has attempted to substantively rein in the military-industrial complex. Eisenhower warned about it, but left it unhindered. John F. Kennedy who had entered office as a stridently militaristic anti-communist in June 1963 spoke of eliminating nuclear arms and liquidating the cold war, thus ushering in an era of peaceful coexistence with the USSR. Five months later he was assassinated. No president, since Kennedy has made a substantive effort to alter the country's imperial thrust and its military arm.

## NeoCons Pushed to the Margins

Obama upon entering office at least tempered the lunacy of Bush's stable of neocon fanatics, substituting his own stable of national security "realists." Obama and his advisors have proposed a foreign and military policy within the framework of traditional imperial interests but reconfigured to meet changing domestic and foreign conditions.

Pressure from the multi-trillion dollar debt has forced the administration to propose slowing the rate of growth of the military over the next ten years (given the leverage of the MIC over Congress one can wonder if this will ever transpire). During that decade $487 billion will be trimmed from military spending, with some big weapons programs canceled. Troops on the ground are to be reduced while drones and other types of cyber warfare along with reservists are to play an expanded role in targeted destruction of would-be enemies. Highly trained (and very lethal) "special operations" forces are to be stressed (like navy SEAL specialist killers) to "sustain US global leadership."

Crucially, Obama and his advisors have abandoned the concept of fighting two simultaneous major ground wars (popular with Bush's neo-cons). However, that does not negate an ambitious military agenda. The plan advanced by the Administration and Pentagon says: "Even when US forces are committed to a large-scale operation in one region, they will be capable of denying the objectives of—or imposing unacceptable costs on an opportunistic aggressor in a second region." Significantly, the new doctrine cannot sustain "long wars" zealously advocated by some in the Pentagon to continue un-winnable low intensity conflicts without end. If Obama is re-elected, we can anticipate that a substantive withdrawal of US forces from Afghanistan (his originally preferred war) will be completed in 2014. That would constitute a win for the peace movements here and around the world.

## The Obama Doctrine

Obama has offered a new strategic doctrine that shifts imperial-military emphasis from Europe to China and Iran that are now at the centers of US "security" concerns. Washington has declared that South Asia and the Pacific are the rising areas of commercial and financial vitality that must remain open to US commerce and investment. Essential to "rebalancing" US forces from Europe, sea-lanes from the Strait of Hormuz to the Indian Ocean to the Pacific are to be protected by large concentrations of US naval forces – not very different in content from standard imperial behavior.

The Administration claims that its strategic "rebalancing" is not aimed at China (and North Korea). But the establishment of a US marine base at Darwin, Australia, a new cozy relationship with the generals in Myanmar (Burma), increased military ties with the Philippines, even efforts to exploit Vietnam's conflicts with China through naval cooperation with the Vietnamese, and of course, continuing US bases in Japan – constitute an effort to virtually encircle China and to challenge Chinese interests in South Asia.

While there is ample evidence that Obama (through Panetta) is pressuring Israel to restrain its desire to attack Iran's nuclear facilities, the Administration nevertheless in an election year is playing a worrisome game with large naval concentrations at the Strait of Hormuz and in the Arabian Sea and with pursuit of extremely painful sanctions on Iran (which, among other things, threaten to send oil prices through the roof, thus undermining a global economic recovery).

The Administration is well aware that Iran is not building a nuclear bomb while the Iranians proceed with a legal nuclear program that can be converted to weapons production if it believes that it is confronted with an "existential threat." Of course, Washington is aware that IAEA inspectors are on the ground in Iran, that Iran (facing Israel's large nuclear arsenal) is again pressing for negotiations (including a nuclear free ME) and that the former head of the Israeli Mossad has flatly stated that even Iranian acquisition of a nuclear weapon would not constitute an "existential threat" to Israel.

## Netanyahu Spells Disaster

Yet, the Netanyahu regime, faced with a domestic "Occupy" movement that to scale is larger than anywhere else, may seek to divert its public from economic grievances by launching an attack on Iran's facilities. There are reports that in an election year, the Administration would not seek to restrain Netanyahu, but would try to distance itself from such an attack. However, if such a situation arises, right wing pressure could well force Obama into a disastrous conflagration. Yet, there is ample evidence that this administration has been, and can be, sensitive to the public's war weariness and its desires for peace. At this political moment stopping an attack on Iran should be the prime priority of peace activists.

The contradictory mix of positive and negative is evidenced in Latin America and the Caribbean. Obama has pressed a free trade agreement with regressive anti-union Colombia while it has loosened the blockade of Cuba.

Of enormous potential is Obama's stated goal of sharply reducing and eventually eliminating all nuclear weapons. The Pentagon's new strategy document projects a major reduction in its nuclear arsenal. Again, that vital goal is undermined by the expenditure of billions to "upgrade" an aging nuclear arsenal. But Obama has opened the door to concrete advances in reducing and ultimately eliminating nuclear weapons. It's up to a growing and energized peace movement to walk through that door and in an Obama second term to register real progress on another "defining issue" of peace or annihilation.

Perhaps the most troubling aspect of Obama's administration is its obeisance to the national security state. The combined "security" structures —the FBI, CIA, NSA (National Security Agency), ICE (Immigration and Customs Enforcement) and now the massive Department of Homeland Security are among the most institutionally rooted agencies in the country's history. Their definition of "security" historically has included odious attempts to suppress constitutional rights of US citizens and immigrants. That compulsion has only increased since 9/11 when the "war on terror" has been brought home with pressure on Muslim communities in particular, including dubious indictments of Muslims; surveillance, grand jury subpoenas and harassment of peace and justice activists; failure to challenge congressional resistance to closing Guantanamo; huge round-ups of undocumented immigrants; and a strong penchant (sometimes eclipsing the Bush administration) for protecting and extending secret operations of the agencies of the national security state.

## Grassroots Defense Needed

It's up to an alert and determined movement to defend the Constitution to say that signing statements disavowing intentions to hold citizens without charge under the NDAA (National Defense Authorization Act) are not enough. It's up to the public to insist that hard-won civil liberties be fully respected.

With all the contradictions in Obama's domestic, foreign, military and security policies, the openings for successful pressure to move in a progressive direction exist—especially in light of a shifting public consciousness largely inspired by Occupy Wall Street.

On the other hand, one need to only briefly contemplate the current Republican field vying for that party's presidential nomination. Never in recent memory has such an unvarnished group of rabid clownish right wing reactionaries been assembled. Their candidacies, fueled by super PACs funded by the most odious elements of the one percent (largely fossil fuel, gambling and personal wealth) offer the most nightmarish political scenario imaginable. One can be reasonably troubled and resistant to aspects of Obama's foreign policy "realism," but the ravings of the Republican field to build an even more gigantic military than the present behemoth, to "regime change" in Cuba, to face down China, to illegally move the US Embassy to Jerusalem, to launch a war against Iran, etc. is more than simple rationality can allow. Nor can our commitment to eradicating racism, sexism and all forms of oppression leave unchallenged the Republicans' assaults on the right to reproductive choice and their crude "dog whistles" aimed at stirring vile anti-Obama racism. Removal of the threat from the right—be it from Romney or Gingrich MUST be the priority of all progressives.

Of course that clearly mandates voting for Obama's reelection. But that is one crucial part of a broader strategy that can be embraced by independent Progressives, Democrats, third party advocates and those forces that eschew electoral politics. That is the strategy of continuing to build and expand grass roots movement to challenge the hegemony of finance capital, the Pentagon and the national security state. It requires working for the progressive program enumerated earlier. It requires solid efforts to defeat the right at the congressional and local elective levels. It requires broad labor and progressive support for OWS that will surely press on with new actions in the spring. It requires mutual regard between those working to rekindle the spirit of "hope and change" within the Obama campaign and those pressing the issues through independent parties. At bottom, the activism of all movements for a progressive response to the continuing economic crisis will have a salutary, vital impact upon the elections. In turn, that movement that has already obliged Obama to alter his rhetoric and address that defining issue of income inequality, can and must come out of this election campaign stronger, clearer and more determined to effect change than ever. That is our sacred duty to present and future generations.

*Mark Solomon is a former National Co-Chair, Committees of Correspondence for Democracy and Socialism*

# The Foreclosure Crisis:
# Urgent as Ever and Could Get Worse

## By Carl Bloice

Noting that a Federal judge in California was slated to soon okay the "largest residential fair-lending settlement in
history" ever reached by the Department
of Justice in a bias case," Attorney Anita
Hill commented in *Time* magazine last
week that in putting together the deal
the U.S. Attorney's office is to be laud-
ed. She added "without Countrywide's
admission of fault for overcharging and
steering minorities into high cost loans
when they qualified for conventional
loans, it's uncertain whether the agreement will stave off future unlawful behavior. Moreover, it certainly won't be

enough to repair the damage that has been done to those individuals
and the communities in which they reside."

The agreement requires Countrywide Financial Corporation - now part
of Bank of America—to pay $335 million to African American and Latino
homeowners who have been found—in Hill's words—"victims of Countrywide's racially motivated fraud and deceit. To begin with, the $10,000
compensation some of the 200,000 Countrywide customers covered in
the settlement are entitled to is likely not enough to put them back
in their homes, let alone rebuild their neighborhoods," Hill wrote. Hill,
author of *Reimagining Equality: Stories of Gender, Race, and Finding
Home*, is a professor of social policy, law and women's studies at Brandeis University.

## Fraud Apparent

That some of the nation's leading banks and mortgage lending institutions were engaged in fraudulent, predatory and discriminatory lending
practices was obvious over four years ago—before it was clear public
knowledge that the distortion they created in the housing market was
central to the country's continuing economic crisis. The devious ways

that major financial institutions went about trading, hiding or escaping responsibility for the mortgage mess they had created lay at the heart of the "great recession" in the U.S., but were also instrumental in the economic difficulties that show no signs of abating in Europe.

The unemployment problem in the country today means depravation and hardship for millions of people. So, too, does the plague of housing foreclosures. So long as it persists, economists say, there is next to no possibility of anything approaching an economic recovery.

"It was 35 years ago that US president Jimmy Carter declared the energy crisis 'the moral equivalent of war.' His use of martial language might not have galvanized Americans in the way he hoped, but it still is useful to think of economic struggles in military terms," wrote the *Financial Times* Lex column January 10. "Today's enemy is the housing crisis and the fight is going badly. Prices are down by a third and there is a glut of foreclosures, with another wave coming. Allowing more foreclosures not only further depresses this pool of wealth but makes it tough to normalize interest rate policy," the column said.

On January 11, the Federal Reserve said the country's housing market remains stagnant. The word it used was "sluggish." Or, as political commentator and former New York governor Eliot Spitzer put it: "... the mortgage crisis continues, depressing the middle class."

There are an estimated 3.5 million seriously delinquent mortgages out there. There were nearly 2.7 million foreclosure filings on about 1.9 million homes last year. That's down from 2007, but it's still about one out of every 69 homes in the country.

Those tracking the data have suggested the number will be higher this year. The reason? The process Attorney Hill described: "The lack of clarity regarding many of the documentation and legal issues plaguing the foreclosure industry means that we are continuing to see a highly dysfunctional foreclosure process that is inefficiently dealing with delinquent mortgages, particularly in states with a judicial foreclosure process," Brandon Moore, the CEO of RealtyTrac, told the McClatchy newspapers.

## No Serious Solutions

And yet, neither the Congress nor the Obama Administration has come up with any measures that would seriously stem the tide of foreclosures. Nor, as Hill pointed out, are there measures that could result in justice or relief for those conned by the financiers, or guarding against the process resuming.

Last year, as mentioned, there were nearly 2.7 million foreclosure filings—which included default notices, scheduled property auctions and bank repossessions —reported on roughly 1.9 million properties. That works out to about one filing for every 69 U.S. homes. That rate and total foreclosure activity in 2011 were at the lowest annual levels since the housing market imploded in 2007. But the decline may be short-lived, as lenders work their way through the backlog of delayed filings stemming from "robo-signing" scandals. "We expect that trend to continue this year, boosting foreclosure activity for 2012 higher than it was in 2011, though still below the peak of 2010," Moore said.

"The Foreclosure Crisis: A Nation in Denial," is the title of a commentary by Bruce Judson on *Huffington Post* January 9, 2012. "As we start the New Year, the executive branch and Congress continue to pretend the gravest risk to our economy and social stability does not exist: the ongoing foreclosure crisis," wrote Judson, entrepreneur-in-residence at the Yale Entrepreneurial Institute and author of It Could Happen Here: America on the Brink. "The financial crisis began with the housing crisis and it will not end until we resolve housing. Government policymakers who seemingly ignore this basic fact are leading the nation to another potential catastrophe."

In 2007, only a few observers were warning of the devastating effect all this was having, especially on African American and Latino communities from one end of the country to the other.

## One in Four Mortgages in Trouble

"Today, an estimated 29 percent of all homes with mortgages are under-water. In addition, at least one respected analyst estimates that a total of 14 million homes will be foreclosed on from 2007 to the end of the crisis," Judson wrote. "This represents a hard-to-imagine one in every four mortgages. With foreclosures increasing, there is now such a looming imbalance of supply and demand that, as the Fed (Federal Reserve Bank) notes, further decreases in home prices are likely. Some believe home price reductions of another 20 percent are likely. This would, in all likelihood, have disastrous consequences on at least three fronts - and ripple effects that are impossible to predict."

According to Judson, "What is shocking is the almost total lack of attention the administration has paid to suffering homeowners. It's hard for me (and apparently Fed Chairman Bernanke) to understand how the administration can possibly hope to revitalize the economy without seriously addressing the overhang of consumer housing debt. Moreover, the failure to address the risk this poses for a broader economic catastrophe borders on the inexcusable."

"If President Obama is serious about saving the middle class and reducing income inequality, the administration needs to be far more aggressive in developing policies to keep homeowners as homeowners. As I have written before, this was one of FDR's central goals in the New Deal. Detailed proposals for addressing this extraordinary risk do exist. However, they will require a determined effort. There are solutions, but they are not simple."

"What is most important right now is that we recognize we are in a lifeboat that will not reach land," wrote Judson. "We need to focus on implementing a meaningful solution to the problem. A clock is ticking and Washington needs to acknowledge that a witching hour is approaching."

Three years ago, with much fanfare, the Obama Administration launched the Home Affordable Modification Program with a target of assisting over 3 million distressed homeowners. As of the end of the year, it is said to have aided somewhere in the vicinity of 750,000. One problem is that it's voluntary and the bankers aren't in a voluntary mood.

Oh, and those other guys running for office?

In their debate, most have ignored the problem. For the presumed front-runner it's apparently a piece of cake, something "the market" can handle all by itself.

Nevada leads the nation in both joblessness and foreclosures. One out of every 16 homes in the state was subject to some type of foreclosure filing in 2011, according to RealtyTrac, an online foreclosure data firm. "Frontrunner Mitt Romney hasn't pandered to struggling Nevada homeowners," Arthur Delany wrote on *Huffington Post* last week. "He told the *Las Vegas Review-Journal* in October he supports the government stepping aside: "Don't try to stop the foreclosure process. Let it run its course and hit the bottom."

"It's not likely Romney will have much more to say on his next visit," wrote Delany. "The candidates didn't talk foreclosure policy in Iowa, even though the state attorney general is leading national foreclosure settlement negotiations with the country's biggest banks. Only Jon Huntsman, who didn't bother to campaign in Iowa, has taken a position on the settlement."

The Huntsman website says the candidate, if elected, would "direct the Department of Justice to take the lead in investigating and brokering an agreement to resolve the widespread legal abuses such as the robo-signing scandal that unfolded in the aftermath of the housing bubble. This is a basic question of rule of law; in this country no one is above the law."

"Because if we actually believed the lie so often told that if we just worked hard and put our noses to the grindstone that we could be just like Mitt then it wouldn't be so bad," wrote Pamela Hilliard Owens on the *Black Liberal Blogger* last week. "But, see, we're not stupid. Because being broke and poor and being stupid are not synonymous.

"Just as an example? We see things like the Countrywide scandal where a huge corporation ripped off thousands of African American and Hispanic homeowners (my guess is none of them were multi-millionaires), charging them more for mortgages than similarly qualified white folks, just because they could. Sure they got dinged $335 million as a penalty, and congrats to US Attorney Eric Holder for at least getting something out of the bastards, even it wasn't near enough. But what about all those families whose lives are now ruined because of Countrywide? Who is going to put them back together and make them whole?"

## Inequity as Social Dynamite

"These are the kind of things that happen when the deck is stacked, which are the kind of things that gave rise to the Occupy movement and many more similar movements around the world that explode when people get fed up with inequity and injustice. But God knows if we could all just live the Life of Mitt?"

"All would be right with the world, wouldn't it, kids?"

"Ultimately, after the financial market collapsed, the government bailed out the banking industry, including Bank of America, which now owns Countrywide," wrote Hill in Time. "The banking industry rebounded because the government concluded that a secure banking system was in the public's interest. Yet, the playing field won't be level as long as American communities pay for the corrupt decisions made by lenders. A federal effort targeted at restoring blighted neighborhoods is needed to clean up the mess left behind by such egregious predatory practices as those alleged in the Department's reports and pleadings."

"... Funding to restore the neighborhoods Holder's team of attorneys, economists and mathematical statisticians have identified would enhance the DOJ's effectiveness as well as assist state and local governments currently dealing with costs associated with these sites. As importantly, it would show our federal government's commitment to the protections enshrined in our Constitution and laws."

"The greed and fraud of Wall Street banks caused the loss of millions of homes and billions of dollars in the housing crash," read a recent statement from MoveOn.org. "Now we need President Obama to take a strong stance for homeowners, and for accountability, by opening a federal investigation into big bank fraud."

"This is something the president can do on his own right now, without fighting Congress. And millions of Americans can be helped if banks are held responsible and forced to compensate homeowners for their wrongdoing."

"Wall Street gets investigated for the misdeeds that led to our financial collapse, they're very worried about what we'll find," read a recent statement by Russ Feingold, founder of Progressives United. "That's why they're eager for a sweetheart settlement deal that would give them broad immunity without an investigation. Thanks in part to the pressure thousands of fellow progressives put on state attorneys general, that deal is on hold."

"But we don't just need to stop a deal that will cut off an investigation - we need President Obama to take the lead and launch the investigation. That's why we're joining with our friends at Move On to petition the president to investigate Wall Street now."

"... For far too long, Wall Street has received a blank check from Washington. They got bailed out after they gambled our economy into a recession, and they lobbied hard to make sure that regulation was too weak to prevent another crash."

"So without an investigation, we can't hold the big banks truly account-able for the $7 trillion they cost the global economy, homeowners can't get fair compensation, and Wall Street will have no reason to stop skew-ing the playing field against the 99%."

## Yet another Task Force

Recently, *The New York Times* called upon the Obama Administration to provide leadership on the matter by appointing "an interagency task force to investigate and pursue potential civil and criminal wrongdoing by institutions and people whose conduct in the mortgage chain had the greatest economic impact," led by "a leader with the impulses of a crusading prosecutor" that would focus its attention on "the large banks and their top echelons."

"Bankers should not be allowed to walk away from the economic havoc they wreaked upon the country," says Robert L. Borosage, co-director of the Campaign for America's Future, "They should be held accountable, so that no one on Wall Street even thinks about playing roulette with people's lives again."

*BlackCommentator.com Editorial Board member Carl Bloice is a writer in San Francisco, a national co-chair of CCDS, and formerly worked for a healthcare union.*

# Whose 'America' Will It Be?
# The Far Right's Assault on
# Mexican-American Studies in Arizona

## By John Crawford

There's a culture war being fought today in the public schools of Tucson, Arizona. As a result of a January 10, 2012 decision by Tucson Unified School District, courses in Mexican American Studies were terminated at mid-month and classroom books were either removed altogether or put under lock and key.

Students have staged citywide demonstrations and embattled educators at the University of Arizona and the local public schools are fighting back. An alternative program of courses is being offered outside school grounds for students willing to attend them without academic credit for the time being. Regional and national support, including teach-ins in many institutions, is being mounted to protest Arizona's refusal to allow indigenous people to learn, or even read, about their own culture in the classroom.

Several days after the January 10 decision, school officials invaded Tucson's high school classrooms while classes were in session, snatched books off the shelves and sometimes out of tearful students' hands, and sent them to storage facilities at unknown locations. The courses themselves were cancelled, the teachers reassigned. The same teachers were called together and warned not to discuss subjects pertaining to racial issues, political resistance, Mexican American culture, or the termination of their own courses, in their remaining classes. Some teachers were subsequently monitored in their classrooms. One teacher was told to avoid assigning Shakespeare's play *The Tempest* because it dealt with such issues as the confinement of the slave Caliban.

Some books were banned, others merely hidden away. Among the books singled out for removal, the following were essential components of the Mexican American Studies program:

*Rethinking Columbus: The Next 500 Years*, by Bill Bigelow *500 Years of Chicano History in Pictures*, Elizabeth Martinez *Critical Race Theory*, by Richard Delgado and Jean Stefancic *Chicano! The History of the Mexican Civil Rights Movement*, by F. Arturo Rosales *Message to Aztlan*, by Rodolfo "Corky" Gonzalez *Occupied America: A History of Chicanos*, by Rodolfo Acuna *Pedagogy of the Oppressed*, by Paolo Freire.

Books removed from the shelves included popular literary works by contemporary Chicano authors Rudolfo Anaya, Sandra Cisneros, Gloria Anzaldua, Jimmy Santiago Baca, Dagoberto Gilb, and Luis Alberto Urrea, and Native American authors Sherman Alexie, Joseph Bruchac, Scott Momaday, and Leslie Silko. Also removed were such schoolroom standards as Thoreau's Civil Disobedience, Howard Zinn's *People's History of the United States*, Jonathon Kozol's *Savage Inequalities*, and James Baldwin's *The Fire Next Time*.

The School District's decision to terminate the program was dictated by the state's threat to withdraw funding for the Tucson district, which it found in violation of state law HB 2281, originally drafted in 2011. The story of the drafting of the law and the political pressure to assure its enforcement goes back at least five years.

## The History OF HB 2281

Early impetus for the attack on Mexican American Studies came in an "Open Letter to the Citizens of Tucson," drafted on June 11, 2007 by Tom Horne, Arizona Superintendent of Public Instruction. The first section of his letter was titled "The Tucson Unified School District Ethnic Studies Program Should Be Terminated." Distorting the facts from the very beginning of his letter, Horne said he believed "it is fundamentally wrong to divide students up according to their racial group and teach them separately." He charged that the Ethnic Studies program "teaches a kind of ethnic chauvinism that the citizens of Tucson should no longer tolerate." He objected to one of the texts, Paolo Freire's *Pedagogy of the Oppressed*, by saying "Those students . . . should not be taught that they are oppressed." He accused another text, *Occupied America: A History of the Chicanos*, by historian Rodolfo Acuna, of "taking the Mexican side of the battle at the Alamo."

Horne warned the citizens of Tucson at the end of his letter that he would continue to "use my pulpit to bring out the facts, but only you can bring about change." Actually he went further than using his "pulpit." In

the next several years, supported by right-wing Arizona politicians, he drafted House Bill 2281 for adoption by the state legislature, beginning with the inflammatory statement "Public school pupils should be taught to treat and value each other as individuals and not be taught to resent or hate other races or classes of people." The bill was passed early in 2010 and went into effect on January 1, 2011—on the same day Horne resigned as Superintendent of Public Instruction to be appointed Arizona State Attorney General, with the power to enforce the legislation.

Actually, the new law was not implemented until a year later, when John Huppenthal, Horne's successor as Superintendent of Education, forced the Tucson United School District to enforce it, on pain of being stripped of state revenues. The major provisions of the law follow a torturous course of development which is strategic rather than logical. They read as follows.

A school district of charter school in this state shall not include in its program of instruction any courses or classes that include any of the following:

*Promote the overthrow of the United States government.

*Promote resentment toward a race or class of people.

*Are designed primarily for pupils of a particular ethnic group.

*Advocate ethnic solidarity instead of the treatment of pupils as individuals. Significantly, the third item forbids a concentration on common ethnicity, while the fourth explicitly forbids solidarity. As has been pointed out, "If this were labor legislation, the fourth item would be a 'right-to-work' clause."

The other significant section of the law deals with conditions for other ethnic studies courses. Believing that the opening statement, above, is sufficient to ban Mexican-American Studies, Horne and the other authors crafted provisions of the law which appear to ACCEPT courses in Native American Studies ("classes . . . that are required to comply with federal Law"); "classes that include the history of any ethnic group and that are open to all students" (EXCEPT Mexican American Studies); "classes that include the discussion of controversial aspects of history" (EXCEPT Mexican American Studies); and "instruction of the Holocaust, any other instance of genocide, or the historical oppression of a particular group of people based on ethnicity, race, or class" (EXCEPT Mexican American Studies). In other words, the entire bill is designed to eliminate ONLY Mexican American studies from the curriculum.

As the legal process ground on, responses were forthcoming from outside Arizona. A meeting of United Nations rapporteurs from the Permanent Forum on Indigenous Issues directed their attention to HB 2281 in May 2010, after it was signed by Governor Jan Brewer but before it was implemented:

Such law and attitudes are at odds with the State's responsibility to respect the right of everyone to have access to his or her own cultural and linguistic heritage and to participate in cultural life.

Such outside objections, however, were not about to impede the work of the authorities in Arizona.

**Another America**

So the target of this classroom "auto de fe," as one of the program organizers called it, was the teaching of Mexican American Studies as an integral part of the Ethnic Studies curriculum. For years, right-wing state politicians had viewed Mexican American Studies as a dangerous breeding ground of anti-American sentiment. What it truly represented was a direct challenge to American Exceptionalism, and a way of claiming a hearing for the indigenous peoples of a major territorial region of the Americas.

While the politicians' xenophobia was also reflected in Arizona's no-
torious anti-immigration legislation bill drafted in the same period, SB
1070 (many students in the Mexican American Studies program also
were subjected to harassment by police when they were stopped without provocation on suspicion of being "illegals"), the ideological thrust
of SB 1070 was directed against Mexican American students and their
families—indeed the entire Mexican American community—as well
as Native Americans throughout southern Arizona who attended the
Mexican American Studies classes and were thought to hold the same
political views.

The core concept of the Mexican American Studies program was to present a history of the people variously called indigenous, red-brown, Chicano, or "Raza" (trans. "the people")—a population base originating in
Mexico and spread to a large section of the American Southwest, the
result of five centuries of continuous migration, cohabitation and cultural fusion.

The program sought to describe the people as they were, whatever their
specific national origins or locations. Central to that description was a
presentation of the common culture, including everything from core my-
thologies, traditional stories, dances and songs, to the daily occupations
of village life—from types of work to the significance of food to medicine
to education.

How could Mexican American Studies be considered so dangerous that
it was something to eliminate? Apparently the greatest danger these
people have represented to the reactionaries of Arizona has been their
self-concept as a people, literally as Raza, since poor people in particular
tend to put that concept first, with any self-identification as "American"
coming in a poor second. In fact, whether educated or not, the indigenous people of the Southwest understand themselves to be essentially
stateless, thriving on the strength of the common culture they have carried inside them for centuries, rather than any national affiliation.

The right-wing legislators who have supported HB 2281 argue that the
word Raza is exclusive (therefore "racist") rather than inclusive. In their
turn, the legislators demand that any political indoctrination of children
in the United States be strictly "American." But "American" seems very
exclusive, in terms of what it implies about both race and class, from
the point of view of La Raza, the indigenous people: and the means of
enforcing the ideology of Americanism in the classroom is absolutely ty-
rannical, a flag-waving version of "My way or the highway." Beyond that,
there is the famous quip by Mexican American dramatist Luis Valdez in
the 1950s: "We didn't discover America, America discovered us."

How odious this situation has been to the Arizona politicians can be seen in the documents they've generated within the last five years about the necessity to convert the indigenous people of the Southwest to the status of loyal Americans. But this dread of cultural difference goes back much further.

### Kiling the Indian

Some of the indigenous people themselves refer to the story of Richard Henry Pratt, Brigadier General of the U.S. Army who was in charge of creating the Indian Schools in the 1880s. In an address to the World Baptist Convention in 1883, General Pratt stated:

> In Indian civilization I am a Baptist, because I believe in
> immersing the Indians in our civilization, and when we get
> them under holding them there until they are
> thoroughly soaked.

More succinctly, General Pratt is remembered for another saying regarding the education of children in his Indian Schools: "Kill the Indian, Save the Man." It has earned him notoriety among Native American peoples to this day.

Arizona, the locus of some of the last Indian wars in the United States and the site of Geronimo's final surrender, has seen La Raza, the mixed-blood inheritors of the Mexican and Indian cultures, much as General Pratt saw his first native students at the Indian School at Carlisle, Pennsylvania. Whenever they were seen merely as human beings, they were considered dispensable. They could justify their existence to the occupiers only when they became "Americanized."

Against this brutal "educational" practice of the colonizer over the colonized, the pedagogical influence of the Brazilian educator Paolo Freire comes into play. Freire's educational goal was essentially stateless: it addressed instead the needs of the student and the goal of creating a just society. Freire noted,

> Education either functions as an instrument which is used
> to facilitate integration of the younger generation into
> the logic of the present system and bring about conformity,
> or it becomes the practice of freedom, the means by which
> men and women deal critically with reality and discover
> how to participate in the transformation of their world.

Having seen this much of the political and historical context of the state of Arizona, we should be surprised no longer that State Superintendent of Education Horne considered Freire a leading enemy in what was, in-deed, a cultural war.

## The Studies Program Fights Back

Long before the Mexican American Studies program was actually sus-pended, it had undertaken a program of promotion and self- defense in case of state attacks.

As the attacks on Mexican American Studies heated up in 2010, the Mex-ican American Studies department of the University of Arizona hosted a "Conference Combatting Hate, Censorship, and Forbidden Curricula" at the University campus on December 2-4, 2010. Organizer Roberto Rodriguez wrote the conference call:

> Everyone is encouraged to learn from the courageous students, educators and community activists that have challenged Arizona's repressive legislation. The challenges have included a summer run from Tucson to Phoenix in 115-degree heat, all-night vigils, walkouts, marches, rallies, protests and mass arrests. At this conference you will be exposed to [both the] research and the experiences of undergraduate and graduate students and faculty and community scholars from throughout Arizona.

The program included the reports of young people who attended classes in the school system. These began with K-6 dialogues between teachers and students. They extended to reports and panels of students currently enrolled in the program and also high school graduates. In the evening, elders and teachers were brought in to dialogue with the more advanced students. Audience discussions were held at the end of each presenta-tion.

Lectures on the second day treated subjects including Indigenous Knowl-edge, Arizona's Neo-Apartheid, Decolonizing the University, Readings from Chicano Studies, Historical Trauma, Beyond Arizona, and Raza Studies: a Science of the People. These presentations revealed the highly developed pedagogical basis of the program.

In the evening, invited guests spoke on several topics: The Battle over SB 1070, Arizona Hate and Homophobia, Raza Studies v. State of Arizona Lawsuit, and The Indigenous Alliance: O'odham (Yaqui Indian) Solidar-ity across Borders. The closing panel, Dialogue: the State of Arizona, included UFW activist Dolores Huerta and Acoma Indian speaker Simon Ortiz.

The third day was given over to culture: a "run/walk" from a nearby mountain to a Tucson community center, followed by talks on the Mexican calendar, presentations of traditional music and dance, and the works of poets and writers. Among the authors contributing to the program were Cherrie Moraga, Francisco Alarcon, and Leslie Marmon Silko.

This event was one of many to be held in Tucson concerning the threat to close down the program. Its public exposure of the history of the struggle and its explanation of the nature of the program pedagogy, together with evidence of the massive support it received from not only the Tucson community but other activists including Native Americans across the state, suggests the scope and influence of this embattled program as a whole.

## The Struggle Continues

After the termination of Mexican American Studies classes and the removal of books from the classrooms was announced January 13, reaction from students, teachers, and the general public was quick in coming. While many outside of Tucson reacted at once to the censorship of books, University of Arizona professor Roberto Rodriguez attempted to clarify the situation at the outset. In an interview on Sunday, January 15, he said, "This is not simply a book-banning; according to Tom Horne, the former state schools superintendent who designed HB 2281, this is part of a civilizational war. He determined that Mexican American Studies is not based on Greco-Roman knowledge and thus lies outside of Western Civilization." Rodriguez compared the confiscation to the Spanish burning of Mayan books in Yucatan 1562: "In that previous era, this would be referred to as reduccion (cultural genocide)."

Immediately the affected students and teachers challenged the termination of classes and banning of books in federal court. Their attorney, Richard Martinez, commented to the press: "Pandora's box has been opened and the ugly face of the bigoted right wing has been exposed for what it is: an attempt to keep Latins poor, dumb, and abused."

Public interest groups were also quick to respond. Rethinking Schools Magazine immediately solicited suggestions from its readers on how to respond to the Tucson action. Its own popular book, *Rethinking Columbus*, had been targeted as a key text in the Mexican American Studies program. On February 1, Rethinking Schools joined in a campaign entitled "No History Is Illegal: A Campaign To Save Our Stories" with the nationally based Teachers Activists Group. More information on their activity is available from either sponsoring group. Librarians' groups have also sought information about banned books, particularly children's books that may have been removed from Tucson school libraries.

*The New York Times* weighed in with a short editorial on Sunday, January 22, in which it said that the Tucson United School District "dismantled its Mexican-American studies program, packed away its offending books, shuttled its students into other classes" because it was "blackmailed into doing so" by the threatened state removal of funding. But the *Times* fell short of suggesting any attempt to restore the suspended program except to hope that Ethnic Studies teachers might rewrite their course descriptions to the school board's approval.

Students from three area high schools walked out of their classes on Monday, January 23 to protest the elimination of the programs. They rallied in front of the School Board offices, after which they were suspended from their schools. They reassembled the next day at a community ballroom for autonomous classes in Ethnic Studies and again the same Thursday to conduct a more structured teach-in and attend Mexican-American Studies classes at the University itself. After Thursday they were told their high school suspensions were lifted.

Teach-ins about the Arizona situation spread across the country. A historians' group circulated reading lists suitable for K-6 children, older students, and the teachers themselves. Teach-ins were held at a number of schools in diverse settings February 1.

A sign-up sheet protesting removal of the books, circulated by Tucson teacher Norma Gonzalez, drew 15,000 signatures. Among those signing were major organizations including the Association of American Publishers, American Association of University Professors, American Booksellers Foundation for Free Expression, National Coalition against Censorship, the National Council of Teachers of English, and the PEN American Center.

Another kind of protest was initiated by an ad hoc group, Librotraficantes, from Houston, Texas. The group plans to mount a book caravan in the middle of March, holding benefit events as they go from Houston to San Antonio, El Paso, Las Cruces (N.M.), Albuquerque, and finally Tucson. They will collect money as they go, use it to pay for pre-purchased copies of confiscated books, and donate the books to the people of Tucson. Some of the affected writers and their independent publishers will join the caravan as it proceeds.

*John Crawford is publisher and editor at West End Press, located in Albuquerque, New Mexico.*

# The Rightwing Agenda in 2012: Medicare, Social Security & Medicaid Still Under Threat

## By Carl Bloice

Next month, people in three Northern California communities will get to see and hear up close former senator Republican Alan Simpson, the man who once referred to Social Security as "a milk cow with 310 million tits," and his trusted sidekick, former White House chief of staff and Morgan Stanley director Democrat, Erskine Bowles.

"Simpson-Bowles" is now a road show. These people never give up.

The duo were appointed by President Obama in February 2010 to co-chair the National Commission on Fiscal Responsibility and Reform, and the sponsors of their March 5-8 Bay Area appearances are promising that they will deliver "a candid, bipartisan discourse on what America's leaders must do to confront the largest and most critical economic, social, business and national security threat that the country faces."

From taxes and spending to entitlement and Social Security reform, Simpson and Bowles "offer an enlightening discussion on solutions for bridging America's deficit, debt and interest gap," the promoters say.

But, as a leader of the local Gray Panthers put it, the two are coming to rally "the 1% for cuts in Social Security, Medicare, and Medicaid, capping all federal revenues, reducing taxes on the rich and increasing them on us, and taxing comprehensive health insurance. As more of us lose jobs and housing, and fall into poverty, B&S are using the deficit as a phony excuse to cut our services and safety net."

The two lecturers are frequently described as responsible for a "deficit-reduction plan put forward by the Simpson-Bowles Commission." Actually no such plan ever existed. The commission met sporadically and the plan drawn up by its staff, which, among other things, targeted Social Security and Medicare for sharp cutbacks-failed to get the support of 14 of the 18 commissioners as required to guarantee they would be taken up by Congress. Exactly how much support the plan had in the panel is unknown because its members never even took a vote.

Following the commission's failure, Simpson and Bowles took the advice of their supporters to "go rogue" and issued the draft report in their own name. It was, and is, only the thoughts of two guys. But the major media took the bait. From then on the country has been treated to endless references to what Richard Haass, president of the Council on Foreign Relations, described as "the comprehensive deficit-reduction plan put forward by the Simpson-Bowles Commission."

Haass surely knows better but then so too should the editors of the usually accurate *Financial Times* who just this last week took President Obama to task editorially saying he had "oddly ignored the findings of the Simpson-Bowles commission he had appointed."

Last March, when Simpson and Bowles first went on tour, Teddy Partridge wrote on firedoglake.com, "There was no actual final report approved by the Cat Food Commission. The Simpson/Bowles commission failed. Their new roll-out press tour is based on a lie."

Why the subterfuge? Why the constant references to a non-extant commission report?

Because the specifics of the proposals pushed by Simpson and Bowles are not really all that important. What they represent is a reference point for what is otherwise known of as the "grand bargain." The essence of the proposals is that there is a trade off involving sharp reductions in programs like Medicare, Social Security and Medicaid in return for changes in tax policy to raise revenue in the face of the federal deficit. Last year, when Congressional Republicans threatened to bring the government to a halt over the routine question of raising the Federal debt limit, Simpson said, "We've got guys who will not approve the debt limit extension unless we give 'em a piece of meat, real meat, off of this package.' And boy the bloodbath will be extraordinary.

## Politics of Debt

Last year, the *Financial Times*, urged the President "to incorporate a sweeping debt reduction proposal in the 'State of Union' address and the White House budget proposal early next year, and begin negotiations with lawmakers on the package."

On November 11, *Washington Post* pundit Kevin Huffman took up what he called "the rogue part of the operation."

"Bowles and Simpson surely released their thoughts because they can't get 14 commissioners to support them and because they certainly can't get either party on board," he wrote. "If they feel strongly about the

*Workers Defending Social Security at a '*
*Blue Dog' Congressional Office*

deficit, they should go totally independent, get some private funding, and engage in the 2012 elections. Demand a balanced budget plan from every national candidate. Release an independent report card of what the deficit will look like for each plan (and run TV ads showing, e.g., 'Sarah Palin's deficit reduction plan: F.') And in case anyone needs a real wakeup call, play some footsie with Mike Bloomberg if, and when, he gets bored in New York."

Something like that appears to have been set in motion.

It's a win-win endeavor for Simpson and Bowles. After 1,200 people showed up to hear them in Durham, North Carolina, John Frank wrote in the (Raleigh) *News & Observer*, "Simpson want to keep the pressure on Congress as they tour the country giving paid speeches about their deficit plan."

You can't buy individual tickets for the Bay Area Simpson Bowles per- formances and the price of the six lectures in the series averages about $400.

## Prepare for Punditry

But you're likely to hear about Simpson-Bowles on more than one evening. The other scheduled speakers are such luminaries as Spencer Wells, Thomas Friedman, David Brooks, David Axelrod, Richard Haass and Michelle Rhee (the only woman in the group being also the only person of color).

Back in October, *New York Times* columnist Friedman criticized President Obama for "refusing to embrace Simpson-Bowles as the basis of a Grand Bargain."

Brooks, another *Times* pundit, has written that "Last fall, the Simpson-Bowles deficit commission released a bold report on how to avoid an economic catastrophe" and "The failure to seize that moment was one of the Obama administration's gravest errors." Brooks was at it again chastising the President saying his address to Congress contained "big, like tax reform or entitlement reform" in a column that began with the words: "The Simpson-Bowles report."

Haass is of the opinion that the Administrations' failure to embrace Simpson and Bowles' ideas are "at odds" with his idea of a "Restoration" agenda the goal of which would be "to rebalance the resources devoted to domestic as opposed to international challenges in favor of the former."

The Simpson Bowles caravansary just might attract special attention around here because of his reference to one of the state's biggest celebrities.

"Alan Simpson, co-chairman of President Barack Obama's debt commission, furthered his penchant for colorful commentary Monday when he unleashed a rambling diatribe targeting what he characterized as a generation of disrespectful youth and their confused grandparents," Nick Wing wrote on the *Huffington Post* last March. "'This is a fakery,' the former Wyoming senator said on Fox News, referring to retirement-age Americans expressing fears about having Social Security funds slashed. "If they care at all about their children or grandchildren, and sometimes I doubt that—I think, you know, grandchildren now don't write a thank-you for the Christmas presents, they're walking on their pants, with the cap on backwards listening to the enema man and Snoopy Snoopy Poop Dogg, and they don't like them!"

On January 25 Josh Gerstein of the *Charleston Gazette* writing on Politico, complained that the President failed to include "The Simpson-Bowles Commission" in this State of the Union address. "Obama did note that he'd 'agreed to more than $2 trillion in cuts and savings,' he wrote, "but he didn't refer to capping domestic spending. He mentioned 'reforms' to 'rein in the long term costs' of popular programs like Medicare and Social Security."

## Cat Food Solution?

"That's all part of the program put forward by the Bipartisan Debt Commission led by Alan Simpson and Erskine Bowles, derided by liberals as the cat food commission. The commission made it into the last two State of the Union speeches. Tuesday, Obama broke the streak."

"So much for the direct plea of Gov. Chris Christie (R-N.J.) - an Obama critic and Mitt Romney endorser - last weekend, Gerstein continued." He could finally embrace Simpson-Bowles," Christie said on NBC's 'Meet the Press.' "That would surprise the nation if he did it, and I think it would show great leadership if the president was willing to do it."

In his recent address, President Obama had this to say: "I'm prepared to make more reforms that rein in the long-term costs of Medicare and Medicaid and strengthen Social Security, so long as those programs remain a guarantee of security for seniors. . . But in return, we need to change our tax code so that people like me, and an awful lot of members of Congress, pay our fair share of taxes."

That's populist sounding but troublingly and short on content and details. Clearly this matter is unsettled. "If offering more reforms leads to benefit cuts for these vital programs then seniors' programs will once again become a bargaining chip traded in exchange for tax breaks millionaires don't need in the first place," warns Max Richtman, President/CEO of the National Committee to Preserve Social Security and Medicare. As the Simpson Bowles traveling show makes clear, the grand bargainers are still at work. Medicare, Social Security and Medicaid—three social advances that have kept millions of working people alive and out of dire poverty—remain threatened. Those who would undermine them have chosen to inject their "reform" notions into the 2012 election campaign. Progressives should take note.

*Carl Bloice is a National Co-Chair of Committees of Correspondence for Democracy and Socialism*

# The New Jim Crow and the Prison-Industrial Complex: The Urgent Case of Howard Morgan

## By Ted Pearson

Democratic forces of the 99 per cent are gathering around the demand for freedom for Howard Morgan. He is the 54 year old African American policeman who was nearly murdered seven years ago by Chicago police on the city's West Side and who was convicted in a 2nd trial late in January this year of four counts of attempted murder of a police officer.

Morgan was shot 28 times by the police, but unlike 23 year old Amadou Diallo who was killed by police in a similar incident in New York in 1999, Morgan miraculously survived. He faces a minimum sentence of 45 years in prison to life without possibility of parole on each count.

According to the only independent eyewitness the police approached his mini-van with guns drawn, pulled him out, threw him to the ground, and opened fire. He never held a gun. According to Morgan himself police took the gun he carries to work. One yelled "gun," and they all opened fire on him.

They shot wildly. The shot Morgan 28 times, his van an uncounted number of times, and furniture and the walls of neighboring apartments. They fired Morgan's own gun in the melee. Two officers were hit by bullets fired by other officers.

Howard Morgan was taken to Mt. Sinai Hospital. Doctors there removed the bullets surgically, and miraculously, he lived. Only three of the bullets were tested to see which gun they had come from. The rest have been "lost."

In roundtable discussions later that day with Assistant State's Attorneys, CPD commanders, and Fraternal Order of Police attorneys the police story took shape: Morgan had attacked them.  He was charged with four counts of attempted murder of the police.

But no gunpowder residue was found on Howard Morgan's hands or clothes.

This case reeks of the kind of white supremacy that shocked the nation 80 years ago when nine Black teenagers were falsely accused and sentenced to death in Scottsboro, Alabama for the rape of two white girls on the flimsiest of evidence.

Peremptory challenges by the prosecution systematically removed most potential Black jurors.  Presiding judge Clayton Crane and prosecutors Daniel Groth and Phyllis Warren, are white. Morgan's attorneys, Randolph N. Stone and Herschella G. Conyers, Professors of clinical law at the University of Chicago are both African American.

The judge and many members of the jury appeared hostile to Morgan and his attorneys.

The jury of 10 whites and 2 African Americans deliberated only 3 hours on a late Friday afternoon, after a trial that heard 9 days of testimony.

Judge Crane refused to allow the jury to hear that 5 years ago Morgan had been acquitted on three of the four charges that he fired his weapon.

Howard Morgan's mini-van, shown riddled with bullets in police evidence photographs, was immediately towed to a scrap yard where it was crushed and completely destroyed.

More than 25 armed, uniformed police officers packed the courtroom on the last day of the trail, intimidating the jury.

The jury ignored contradictions in the testimony of the police about the incident. They said that Morgan had been driving with his lights off; all the police photos show the van lights on. Some said Morgan lay on the ground on his face, handcuffed behind him. Others said he was on his back handcuffed in front.

One of the police testified that he stood over Morgan's prostrate body, shot him twice in the back and beat him in the head, after all other shooting had stopped.

The prosecution's behavior was consistent with racist attitudes toward the Black community. They justified the police actions by repeatedly and

*Howard Morgan*

pointedly characterizing the Lawndale community as an all-Black neighborhood with a high crime rate.

This case calls for the same level of national and international outrage that ultimately saved the lives of the Scottsboro Nine. People who care about democracy and fairness will demand that Howard Morgan be freed immediately on bail, that he get a new trial, or that the ridiculous charges against him be dropped.

## Far Deeper Issues

But this is just a leading edge of a growing movement against the prison-industrial complex that has been the main instrument of the ruling class in re-imposing Jim Crow segregation on Black communities across the country. It is part of the movement that unites the struggle for freedom for Mumia Abu Jamal and Leonard Peltier with the campaign against police torture and other crimes in Chicago, where two men committed suicide in police lockups on the South Side late last year, and where over a hundred men of color were imprisoned after they were tortured by police and forced to confess to crimes.

Michelle Alexander, in her seminal work on "The New Jim Crow: Mass Incarceration in the Age of Colorblindness," clearly documents how the criminal justice system works to impose a new Jim Crow on U. S. society. She dramatically shows how the "war on drugs" launched by Ronald Reagan was part of a "southern strategy" by which working class voters could be split and fooled into voting for right wing white supremacist elements. These elements had been weakened by the Civil Rights Movement and this was their ticket back to supremacy.

But there is a deeper truth here. Alexander notes that "In each generation, new tactics have been used for achieving the same goals – goals shared by the Founding Fathers. Denying African Americans citizenship was deemed essential to the formation of the original union. Hundreds of years later, America is still not an egalitarian democracy. The arguments and rationalizations that have been trotted out in support of racial exclusion and discrimination in its various forms have changed and evolved, but the outcome has remained largely the same. An extraordinary percentage of black men in the United States are legally barred from voting today, just as they have been throughout most of American history. They are also subject to legalized discrimination in employment, housing, education, public benefits, and jury service, just as their parents, grandparents, and great-grandparents once were. We have not ended racial caste in America; we have merely redesigned it."

But a thinking person who cares about justice will have to ask, "How can this happen, time and time again?" It is fairly easy to observe, if one is objective, that "Racism .... rests on the systematic elaboration of the notion of white superiority. And this notion has its origins in and is sustained by racist practices and structures that confine people of color to a subordinate status relative to white people in nearly every area of life."

But this needs to be explained and developed very concretely. We need to find creative ways to disabuse white working class people of the notion that whiteness offers them some kind of privileged position vis-à-vis capitalism. Such notions are instruments of their own exploitation and pits them against their brother and sister workers of color. Capitalism has developed institutions of white supremacy in which white racial privilege appears as a reality relative to people of color. The criminal justice system and the prison-industrial complex are the main instrument, today, by which the 1 per cent maintains white supremacy and its ideas. This saps the strength of the working class and the rest of the 99 per cent in confronting the 1 per cent. To fully grasp the meaning of this we have to examine our history.

## Central Throughout History

Struggles of African Americans in the United States have been a central issue in every juncture of our history. This was true in 1776, when slaveholders rebelling against the threat of British abolitionism were part of the American Revolution and the British were able to use this to their advantage. It was true in the U. S. Civil War. It was a factor in the movement for women's suffrage. It's been a constant theme in the Labor Movement.

Concessions to white supremacy weakened the progressive majority during the New Deal period, and hurt the global war to defeat fascism. These problems continue today in every popular mass movement.

White supremacy is at its root Black oppression. This not a quantitative question of "who is the most oppressed?" It is a qualitative, historically determined question of "Whose oppression is and has been at the center of all struggles?"

Many other peoples of color have suffered and continue to suffer special oppression under U. S. capitalism. These are all manifestations of white supremacy, and they all must be fought.

The genocide against Native Americans (up to total extinction of some peoples and cultures) and the theft of virtually all their land are extreme. The grinding poverty and destruction of Native Americans continues in the shadows of the U.S. society and economy today.

The number of Latin American immigrants in the U. S., their struggles for basic rights, and their role in the working class has grown many times over in the recent past. All Latinos have become a lightning rod for unrelenting attacks by the far right.

Since 9-11 Arab Americans and Muslims of all nationalities have been singled out for harassment, violations of civil liberties, and general discrimination by the government and the far right.

But it is uniquely the continuing legacy of African enslavement—the identification of blackness with inferiority and whiteness with its opposite—that persists and potentially disrupts every political and economic struggle in the United States today, whether it be for a living wage, for civil liberties, for the right to organize, for education and health care, for gender equality, for equal rights of immigrants, for "fair" taxation of wealth, for human rights of gay, lesbian and transgender people—everything.

## Criminal Justice System as Opinion Shaper

The main instrument for perpetuating this social construction of white supremacy today is the criminal justice system. It is not accidental that the majority of the men and women in prison today are African American, and most of the rest are Latino. The so-called criminal justice system and the prison-industrial complex maintain a new form of slavery. It is the primary instrument that enforces the renewed system of jim crow-de facto segregation of Black people throughout the United States today, as documented by Alexander.

The historical record shows that the rape and enslavement of Africa and Africans have been central in modern world history. Karl Marx noted that from its beginnings capitalism was fueled and consolidated by "[t]he discovery of gold and silver in America, the extirpation, enslavement and entombment in mines of the aboriginal population, the beginning of the conquest and looting of the East Indies, the turning of Africa into a warren for the commercial hunting of black skins. ... Capital comes dripping from head to foot, from every pore, with blood and dirt" (Karl Marx, *Capital*, Vol. I, Ch.XXXI, p.703-712, Progress Publishers, Moscow). Unlike the indigenous and aboriginal peoples of the Americas and Asia who were forced into labor on their own soil, early capitalism made Africans into commodities (slaves) and sold them in the Americas. The thousands who died in the Middle Passage were simply spoilage in the view of the slave traders.

Africa was robbed of its most precious resource—its people. Unlike wage workers, whose labor power was purchased as a commodity and whose product was taken, the entire physical existence of Africans was stolen and sold outright. Being African became, as a matter of law and custom, a mark of being a slave, an item for sale in toto as a commodity. The value of this commodity accrued completely to the slave master with nothing for the slave. In contrast, being white became the mark of being free, a vessel of labor power. Free white workers owned themselves and they could sell their labor power as a commodity or not, for their own benefit. Between Black and white was erected a spectrum of color in which one's status as pariah could be determined by the darkness of one's complexion. This spectrum is maintained today by a constant stream of propaganda through news media and entertainment featuring stereotyped Black men and women as criminal, violent, sexually uncontrolled, and totally irresponsible.

How did this idea of racial superiority come into being? Certainly in our creation there was no separation of human beings into categories of free and slave, better or worse, defined by skin color. White supremacy did not "just happen" naturally. Capitalism was its midwife with all the brutality and violence that it brought into the world.

## The Invention of the White Race

The history of how the English colonial masters created and institutionalized white supremacy in their colonies in the Americas is brilliantly documented in detail in Theodore Allen's two volume work, "The Invention of the White Race." Starting in 1616 (before the Pilgrims came to New England) the English shipped thousands of English, Scotch, and Irish to the tobacco plantations of Virginia, where they were held to unpaid work in bondage under contracts typically lasting seven years. They were drawn from among the former peasants cast off the land in the British Isles in the 17th century through the enclosure of the commons and the expropriation of their land. Cast onto the roads, driven into the cities these men and women were arrested en mass for vagrancy, which was made illegal. They were given a choice - prison or Virginia. Work in the tobacco plantations of Virginia was hard and conditions were harsh; most did not live long enough to complete their bondage. Marriage was not permitted among them; fornication was absolutely prohibited.

Some Africans were also brought to Virginia as bonded or indentured workers on the tobacco plantations. They were a minority of such workers originally.

The Virginia Company's plantations were on land that had been taken from its original indigenous inhabitants through force, some of whom struck back. Colonial masters made certain that it was bonded workers, virtual slaves, who bore the brunt of these counter-attacks. In 1676 a frontier planter named Nathaniel Bacon demanded protection against Indian raids from the colonial administration. Failing to get it, he organized an armed force of bonded workers without regard for color or ethnicity, and stormed Jamestown, the seat of power, burning it down.

It may seem ironic that it was in a demand for more aggressive action against the peoples of the First Nations of the new world that Bacon's Rebellion was born. But this was the logic of colonialism.

In 1662, the Virginia House of Burgesses had declared that as a matter of law "all children born in this country shall be held bond or free only according to the condition of the mother." But this condition was not color or ethnically based. In the years after quelling the insurrection Virginia passed racial slavery into law. In 1682 the House of Burgesses declared that "all servants [...] which shall be imported into this country either by sea or by land, whether Negroes, Moors [Muslim North Africans], mulattoes or Indians who and whose parentage and native countries are not Christian at the time of their first purchase by some Christian [...] and all Indians, which shall be sold by our neighboring Indians, or any other trafficking with us for slaves, are hereby adjudged, deemed and taken to be slaves to all intents and purposes any law, usage, or custom to the contrary notwithstanding." Finally, in 1705, they passed the Virginia Slave Code which codified the slavery of all non-Christian servants and declared them and their offspring to be "real estate" and slaves forever.

In his 1625 Essay No. 15, Sir Francis Bacon (a distant cousin of Nathaniel), advised that "a wise government ... can hold men's hearts by hopes, when it cannot by satisfaction." Bacon further noted that "Generally, the dividing and breaking of all factions and combinations that are adverse to the state, and setting them at distance, or at least distrust, amongst themselves, is not one of the worst remedies" for sedition and insurrection. Following Sir Francis' dictum, under the 1705 Virginia Slave Code bonded and free Christian whites were afforded special privileges and exemptions under the law. The contracts of white bondsmen could end; whites received "freedom dues" or grants of grain and land upon obtaining their liberty; Africans and their children, even when the product of rape by their masters, were never to be released from bondage. African Americans could not testify against a white person. Free African Americans could not vote. A slave who defended him or herself against a white person was to be executed. The murder of an African American was not a crime (although repeated abuse of slaves was penalized, much the way we treat animal abusers today).

Being European and "white" was established as a de facto and de jure mark of being free, or potentially free; having a black skin was the mark of the un-free. The white race and white supremacy were invented, and the working population, most of which was European at that time, became easier to control. Allen puts it precisely in his discussion of the revision of the Virginia Slave Code of 1705:

> "The exclusion of free African Americans from the intermediate stratum was a corollary of the establishment of the 'white' identity as a mark of social status. If the mere presumption of liberty was to serve as a mark of social status for masses of European-Americans without real prospects of upward social mobility, and yet induce them to abandon their opposition to the plantocracy and enlist them actively, or at least passively, in keeping down the Negro bond-laborers with whom they had made common cause in the course of Bacon's Rebellion, the presumption of liberty had to be denied to free African Americans".

Another law mandated that pastors were to review the rights of white people and the lack of rights of Black people every Sunday at church.

## Race and Its Myths

The perpetuation of the myth of the white "race" and its presumption of freedom and social mobility continues to infect social and class struggles to this day, even as thousands of white working people are thrown out of work and pushed into homelessness and poverty. No matter how bad things get whites are supposed to find solace in the fact that they are "not black"—because for a majority of African Americans economic depression has been a constant for decades.

Even though there has been progress as a result of the historic civil rights struggles of recent decades, it remains true that the skilled trades in offices and industry are dominated by white men. In spite of progress among many white workers in cutting through the fog of white supremacy, racism still fuels the vitriol heaped upon President Obama by the Faux News-Tea Party right.

Winning the labor movement to struggle against white supremacy has to be a central theme of the class struggle. But this is a very concrete question. Rank and file trade unionists and their leaders need to respond to and join the demand for freedom for Howard Morgan, Mumia Abu Jama, Leonard Peltier, and other victims of racist and political repression. The New Movement called for by Michelle Alexander is taking shape within the Occupy movement and its counterparts.

But fully rejecting white supremacy and confronting the criminal justice system that it now perpetuates it is a major challenge. White supremacy is maintained by practices and institutions in every aspect of American life. An individual white person cannot shed white supremacy by simply denouncing and rejecting "white privilege" in words, or adopting a monastic life style. It can only be fought by living a life of struggle rooted in the knowledge that it is absolutely true that "an injury to any one is an injury to all," or, as the Socialist Eugene Debs put it, "While there is a lower class, I am in it, while there is a criminal element, I am of it, and while there is a soul in prison, I am not free."

White progressives have a duty to set an example in this struggle and to never succumb to the notion that their whiteness imbues them with any superiority. It requires that the fight for the unity of Black and white be constant and in every struggle, never postponed until conditions are "favorable." It requires that progressive white people fight for leadership by African Americans in every movement and struggle, along with that of white workers and Latinos, and women, and for unity of all.

Free Howard Morgan!
Free Mumia Abu Jamal!
Free Leonard Peltier!
Free ALL political prisoners!
Abolish Jim Crow and the Prison-Industrial Complex!

***Ted Pearson is a member of the National Executive Committee, CCDS, and Co-Chairperson of the Chicago Alliance Against Racist and Political Repression***

Introducing....

# THE ONLINE UNIVERSITY OF THE LEFT

A Left Unity Project initiated by CCDS

The OUL is about radical education with a range of ideas, but unabashedly anchored in Marxism. Karl Marx's ideas are a common touchstone for many people working for change. His historical materialism, his many contributions to political economy and class analysis, all continue to serve his core values--the self-emancipation of the working class and a vision of a classless society. There are naturally many trends in Marxism that have developed over the years, and new ones are on the rise today. All of them and others who want to see this project succeed are welcome to take part.

Our aim is to have a full curriculum, hundreds of faculty and tens of thousands of students. There are many courses you can take for free in your own time, alone or with a group. If you are a student in a study group or organizing a forum, with a laptop and projectors you can pick from hundreds of videos, slide shows and other resources on many subjects—science, history, religion, culture and political economy—and use them directly to supplement your discussions.

If you are a teacher, we invite you to enhance our resources. You can join a growing core of faculty, already at 50, and add the links to the course materials and class outlines you may already have posted on the web. If they are not posted, we can do it for you.

The OUL is mostly free. At some point soon, when we deliver lectures in real time, with the ability of students to ask questions and deliver comments via videoconferencing, we will have a small subscription fee for this component.

We're open for more suggestions and your participation. Visit us at http://ouleft.org Send email queries to Carl Davidson: carld717@gmail.com

# *We Need You....*

We're inviting you to join the Committees of Correspondence for Democracy and Socialism. We need your help in building a progressive majority for peace, justice and equally—and then pushing on to a new society where these will be the rule, rather than the exception. Socialism is being more widely discussed today than any time since the 1960s, and you can't take part in it fully without a socialist organization.

Working with many others, CCDS aims to end existing wars and prevent new ones. We oppose the current austerity being imposed upon the working people, a burden made even heavier by militarism and the hidden costs of non-renewable energy systems. We need a global order based on peaceful relations among nations, mutual respect and human rights, and the creation of economies that can exist in harmony with nature.

You can make a difference. Lend a hand in organizing with others to fight for a progressive agenda in the streets, workplaces, communities of faith and schools. It's not crowded up front, so sign up today!

Fill out and mail today.*
❑ Yes, I'd like to join the CCDS. Enclosed is my check for $ _____.
❑ I'd like a subscription to Dialogue & Initiative. Enclosed is my check for $10 ($5 for CCDS members).
❑ I know good causes need money. Here is my contribution of $ ____.

Name _____
Address _____
City _____ State _____ Zip _____
Phone_____ Email _____

Make check payable to Committees of Correspondence, and mail to:
Committees of Correspondence
220 East 42nd St, Suite 407
New York, NY 10017-5806

Phone (212) 868-3733 Email: national@cc-ds.org Web: www.cc-ds.org

* The Committees of Correspondence for Democracy and Socialism (CCDS) is a national organization dedicated to the struggle for justice, equality, democracy, peace and socialism. The annual membership is $36 for individuals; $18 for unemployed, seniors, youth, and others with low income; $48 for households